GRADE
5
AGES 10-11

SCORE!
Mountain
Challenge

**MATH
WORKBOOK**

KAPLAN

PUBLISHING

New York

Contributing Editor: Justin Serrano
Editorial Director: Jennifer Farthing
Editorial Development Manager: Tonya Lobato
Assistant Editor: Eric Titner
Production Editor: Dominique Polfliet
Production Artist: Creative Pages, Inc.
Cover Designer: Carly Schnur

Published by Kaplan Publishing, a division of Kaplan, Inc.
888 Seventh Ave.
New York, NY 10106

Printed in the United States of America

May 2007
10 9 8 7 6 5 4 3 2 1

ISBN-13: 978-1-4195-9457-1
ISBN-10: 1-4195-9457-5

Kaplan Publishing books are available at special quantity discounts to use for sales promotions, employee premiums, or educational purposes. Please email our Special Sales Department to order or for more information at kaplanpublishing@kaplan.com, or write to Kaplan Publishing, 888 Seventh Avenue, 22nd Floor, New York, NY 10106.

Table of Contents

Are you ready for a fun and challenging trip up *SCORE!* Mountain?

Getting Started

This exciting, interactive workbook will guide you through 6 unique base camps as you make your way up *SCORE!* Mountain. Along the way to the top you will have the opportunity to challenge yourself with over 150 math questions, activities, and brain busters as you work towards conquering *SCORE!* Mountain.

To help you figure out the answer to each question, use the blank space on the page or the extra pages at the back of your workbook. If you need extra space, use a piece of scrap paper.

Base Camp

SCORE! Mountain is divided into 6 base camps—each covering an essential math topic—and is aligned to the educational standards set forth by the National Council of Teachers of Mathematics. The final base camp in this workbook, Everyday Math, has a special focus on the many ways we might use math each day.

Your trip through base camp will take you through 19 questions related to the base camp topic, a Challenge Activity designed to give your brain an extra workout, and a 5-question test to see how much you've learned during your climb.

Each question comes with helpful hints to guide you to the right answer. Use these hints to make your climb up *SCORE!* Mountain a successful learning experience!

The Answer Hider

We encourage you to give each question your best effort before looking at the answer; that's why your *SCORE! Mountain Challenge Workbook* comes equipped with a handy answer hider. Tear out the answer hider at the back of this workbook and, while you work on each question, use your answer hider to cover up the solution until you're finished. Then, uncover the answer and see how well you did!

Celebrate!

At the end of each base camp, there's a fun celebration as a reward for successfully making it through. It's the perfect opportunity to take a break and refresh yourself before tackling the next base camp!

SCORE! Mountain Challenge Online Companion

Don't forget—more fun awaits you online! Each base camp comes with a set of 10 online questions and interactive activities, plus a mountain-climbing study partner who will encourage you and help you track your progress as you get closer to the top of *SCORE!* Mountain.

SCORE! online base camps are designed to supplement the educational themes of each base camp from the book. As you reach the end of each base camp in the book, we encourage you to go to your computer to round out your *SCORE!* Mountain Challenge experience. Plus, after you successfully complete the last online base camp, you are awarded a Certificate of Achievement.

Certificate of Achievement

Upon completion of the entire book and online program, you will receive your very own Certificate of Achievement that can be shared with family and friends!

Time Management

In addition to all of the great math practice that your *SCORE! Mountain Challenge Workbook* has to offer, you'll find an array of helpful tips and strategies at the front of the workbook on how you can best organize and manage your time to stay on top of your busy schedule, do well at school, get all of your homework and chores done, and still have time for fun, family, and friends! It's a great way to help you perform at your best every day!

Tools

Every mountain climber needs a set of tools to help him or her reach the mountaintop! Your *SCORE! Mountain Challenge Workbook* has a special set of tools for you. In the back of your book you'll find a handy guide to help you get through each base camp. Turn to the back of the workbook and use these tools whenever you need a helping hand during your climb up *SCORE!* Mountain.

Enjoy your trip up *SCORE!* Mountain. We hope that it's a fun and educational learning experience!

GOOD LUCK!

Being organized and managing your time well are very important skills to learn. They are a valuable key to success!

Here are some tips to help.

Getting Started

- *Be realistic.* We all wish that we had an endless number of hours in the day to take care of all of our responsibilities and still have time for all of the fun things we want to do. The truth is that every person in the world has the same amount of time to work with. Each of us gets 24 hours a day, 7 days a week, so how you budget your time is important!

- *Keep a schedule.* To help keep track of your time, try creating a weekly schedule. You can use a calendar or organizer, or you can make your own schedule on a blank piece of paper. Your weekly schedule might look like this:

My Weekly Schedule

	MON.	TUES.	WED.	THURS.	FRI.	SAT.	SUN.
6:00 A.M.							
7:00 A.M.							
8:00 A.M.							
9:00 A.M.							
10:00 A.M.							
11:00 A.M.							
12:00 P.M.							
1:00 P.M.							
2:00 P.M.							
3:00 P.M.							
4:00 P.M.							
5:00 P.M.							
6:00 P.M.							
7:00 P.M.							
8:00 P.M.							
9:00 P.M.							
10:00 P.M.							

- *Budget time*. Set aside time on your schedule for all of your regular daily activities. For instance, if you go to school between 7:00 A.M. and 2:30 P.M. each weekday, write that on your schedule. Be sure to include any important chores, responsibilities, after-school clubs, and special events. Budget time for homework and school assignments as well, but also make time for fun with your friends and family!

Staying Organized:

- *Write it down*. The best way to keep track of new activities or assignments is to write them down. Whenever something new comes up, add it to your schedule!

  You can also try keeping a "To Do" list to make sure you remember everything. Try to estimate the amount of time it will take to complete your assignments. It's a good way to budget your time!

- *Have a daily plan*. Each day, plan out what chores, assignments, and activities you have to do that day. Use your "To Do" list to help. Some activities may take up more time, so make sure you have enough time that day to complete everything. Your daily plan might look something like this:

Sample Daily Plan

MONDAY	
6:00 A.M.	Get up, get dressed
7:00 A.M.	Eat breakfast Go to school
7:40 A.M.	School starts
2:30 P.M.	School ends Karate Club meeting – gym
3:30 P.M.	Get home from school
4:00 P.M.	Homework, and chores (see "To Do" list)
6:30 P.M.	Dinner
7:30 P.M.	Call friends and watch TV
8:45 P.M.	Get ready for bed
9:00 P.M.	Bed

Doing Homework

- *Set homework time.* Your schedule should include a block of time for doing homework. If possible, make this block of time for right after you get home from school, so you're sure to have enough time to complete your assignments. How much time do you usually need for homework? Write that on your weekly schedule.

- *Get right to it!* When it's time to do your homework, stay focused. Try to work straight through until you get it done. You'll be happy to finish, so you can move on to other fun things! Sometimes a small, healthful snack can help keep you going and energized!

- *Stay organized.* Set up your homework space in a well-lit area with all the things you'll need to do a great job. This includes your schoolbooks, a dictionary, a calculator, pens, and extra paper. If you keep these items handy, it makes learning a lot more organized and fun!

- *Improve your skills.* Good students develop their skills both inside and outside the classroom. Your *SCORE! Mountain Challenge Workbook* can help. Set aside part of your homework time each day for completing sections from the workbook. Check your progress with the online quizzes as well.

Chores and Activities

- *Keep your commitments.* Remember to include your chores in your daily schedule. You might even set aside a "chore time." Be sure to include chores on your daily "To Do" list as well.

- *Know your limits.* How many school activities can you manage? Be realistic when you join clubs or sign up for activities. Activities are fun, but you must make time for all of the other things going on in your life.

- *Set priorities.* If you don't have many commitments, you can get everything done in your free time. But what if you're committed to more things than you have time for? Then you must set priorities.

  A **priority** is something that's important to you. When you set priorities, you choose the items from your list that are most important to complete.

Use the worksheet below to help you determine your priorities.

Priorities Worksheet

Review the list of activities below. Write your own activities in the blank spaces next to Clubs, Sports, and Classes. Add any other activities on the lines next to Other.

In the column marked Priority, give each activity a letter: **A**, **B**, or **C**:
- **Priority A** = very important to me
- **Priority B** = important to me
- **Priority C** = less important to me

Priority	Activity	Priority	Activity
_____	Homework _____	_____	Sports _____
	_____	_____	_____
_____	Chores _____	_____	Other _____
_____	_____	_____	_____
_____	Clubs _____	_____	_____
_____	_____	_____	_____
_____	Classes _____	_____	_____
_____	_____	_____	_____

List your top 5 priorities below. These items are the most important to you. You should always focus on getting these done.

Priority	Activity
1	
2	
3	
4	
5	

Once you know what's important to you, make sure the things that are top priority get done first!

Setting Goals

- **Even though you're busy, it's also great to try new things Setting goals will help you with this!**

- Maybe you want to try a new sport, join a new club at school, or read a new book. Fill in the spaces below to help you get started reaching your goals. Every time you reach a goal, make a new goal for yourself. You'll be amazed at how much you can do!

What is your #1 goal?

_____

_____

How are you going to reach your #1 goal?

_____

_____

Leaving Time for Fun!

- Everyone needs time to relax and recharge. Include some time in your schedule for relaxing and just having fun with your family and friends. You'll be glad you did!

Your *SCORE! Mountain Challenge Workbook* comes with a fun, interactive online companion. Parents, go online to register your child at **kaptest.com/scorebooksonline**. Here your child can access 60 exciting math activities and a cool mountain-climbing study partner.

Children, when you log on, you'll be brought to a page where you will find your *SCORE! Mountain Challenge Workbook* cover. You'll also be asked for a **password**, which you will get from a passage in this workbook. So have your workbook handy when you're ready to continue your *SCORE!* Mountain Challenge online, and follow the directions.

Good luck and have fun climbing!

Base Camp

Number Sense

Are you ready to begin climbing *SCORE!* Mountain? Let's get started! Good luck!

SCORE! MOUNTAIN TOP

BASE CAMP 5

BASE CAMP 4

BASE CAMP 3

BASE CAMP 2

BASE CAMP 1

1. How many **prime numbers** are **less than 30**?

Write your answer on the line below.

_____

Hint #1:

A **prime number** is a whole number whose only factors are 1 and itself. For example, there are only two whole numbers that can be multiplied together to equal 5: $5 \times 1 = 5$. Therefore, 5 is a prime number.

Hint #2:

You can make an organized list, starting with 2, the smallest and only even prime number. Then, continue with the next larger prime numbers: 3, 5, 7…Stop when you get to the largest prime number smaller than 30.

Answer: There are **10** prime numbers that are less than 30.

The list of prime numbers less than 30 are: **2**, **3**, **5**, **7**, **11**, **13**, **17**, **19**, **23**, and **29**.

2. Which of the following **number sets** lists all the **factors of 12**?

    Ⓐ {0, 12, 24, 36}

    Ⓑ {1, 2, 6, 12}

    Ⓒ {1, 2, 3, 4, 6, 12}

    Ⓓ {1, 2, 3, 4, 6, 8, 12}

Hint #1:

Factors are the whole numbers that divide into another number without leaving a remainder. The factors of 12 will be **equal to** or **less than 12**.

Hint #2:

When looking at the sets of numbers to choose from, make sure each of the numbers in the set are actual factors of 12 and there are no extra numbers in the set.

Answer: The correct answer is choice **C**.

Choice **A** lists multiples of 12, or numbers that are the result of multiplying 12 by a whole number. Choice **B** lists some of the factors of 12, but is missing the factors 3 and 4. Choice **D** lists all the factors of 12, but also includes 8, which is not a factor of 12.

3. Circle the **composite number** in the list below.

 2   3   5   9

Hint #1:

A **composite number** has **more than two factors**. Look for a number that has more than just one pair of factors.

Hint #2:

You are looking for a number that is **not** a prime number. A prime number has exactly two factors, 1 and itself. Find the number that has at least one factor other than 1 and the number itself. Remember that 2 is the smallest and only even prime number.

Answer: The correct answer is **9**.

The number 9 has three factors. These are numbers that will divide into 9 without leaving a remainder.

The factors of 9 are **1**, **3**, and **9**, so 9 is a composite number.

4. Can you help Rosalyn determine which of the following numbers is larger? Circle your choice.

thirty-two thousand twenty-eight

or

thirty-two thousand two hundred eight

Hint #1:

Write out each number in **numerical form**.

Hint #2:

After writing them out in numerical form, compare the two numbers by looking at place values.

Answer: **Thirty-two thousand two hundred eight** is the larger number.

To compare the numbers, start from the left and compare each place value. Since each number starts with **32 thousand**, compare the digits following the commas.

In the first number, the value of these three places is **28**.
In the second number, the value of these three places is **208**.
Since **208** is larger than **28**, then **32,208** is larger than **32,028**.

5. Which of the following lists of numbers is correctly ordered from **least** to **greatest**?

Ⓐ 16,024; 16,204; 16,240

Ⓑ 16,204; 16,024; 16,240

Ⓒ 16,240; 16,024; 16,204

Ⓓ 16,024; 16,240; 16,204

Hint #1:

Look at the **place value** of the numbers in the answer choices. Since each of the numbers in the choices start with 16 thousand, look at the **hundreds** and **tens** places to determine the correct order.

Hint #2:

Compare the three digits after the comma in each number. Place these numbers in order from smallest to largest to help you find the correct answer choice.

Answer: The correct answer is choice **A**.

16,024 is less than **16,204**, and **16,204** is less than **16,240**.

6. What is the **least common multiple** of 8 and 12?
Write your answer below.

_____

Hint #1:

The **least common multiple** is the smallest number that **both 8** and **12** will divide into without leaving a remainder.

Hint #2:

Make a list of the **multiples of 8** and the **multiples of 12**. Multiples are found by multiplying the number by other whole numbers. An example of the multiples of **8** are **8 × 1 = 8, 8 × 2 = 16, 8 × 3 = 24**, and so on. Then search the lists for the smallest number common to both lists.

Answer: The least common multiple of 8 and 12 is **24**.

Multiples of 8 are **8, 16, 24, 32, 40**…
Multiples of 12 are **12, 24, 36, 48**…
The **smallest number** that is on both lists is **24**.

7. What is the **greatest common factor** of 18 and 24?
Write your answer below.

_____

Hint #1:

The **greatest common factor** is the largest number that will divide into **both 18** and **24** and **not** leave a remainder.

Hint #2:

List all the factors of **18** and all the factors of **24**. Then find the **largest** number that is common to both lists.

Answer: The greatest common factor of 18 and 24 is **6**.

Factors of 18 are **1, 2, 3, 6, 9,** and **18**.
Factors of 24 are **1, 2, 3, 4, 6, 8, 12,** and **24**.
Even though 1, 2, and 3 are also in both lists, the greatest number common to both lists is **6**.

8. Can you help Nicholas write the fraction $\frac{12}{16}$ in its **simplest form**? Write your answer on the line.

_____

Hint #1:

To write a fraction in **simplest form**, the numerator (top number) and denominator (bottom number) need to become **as small as possible**. At the same time, the new fraction must be **equivalent** to the fraction stated in the question.

Hint #2:

Look for the greatest common factor of **12** and **16**. Divide the numerator and denominator each by that number. The result will become the fraction in simplest form.

Answer: The fraction $\frac{12}{16}$ in simplest form is $\frac{3}{4}$.

To simplify, divide the numerator and denominator by their greatest common factor. $\frac{12 \div 4}{16 \div 4} = \frac{3}{4}$

9. Which of the following is **true**?

(A) $\frac{3}{4} > \frac{1}{2}$

(B) $\frac{1}{2} < \frac{1}{3}$

(C) $\frac{2}{3} > \frac{3}{4}$

(D) $\frac{1}{4} < \frac{1}{6}$

Hint #1:

This question compares different fractions using the symbols > (**greater than**) and < (**less than**). **Convert** each fraction so that it has the **same denominator** and use the numerators to compare the values. When fractions have common denominators, the larger the numerator the greater the fraction.

Hint #2:

When changing to a **common denominator**, first find the **least common multiple** of the denominators. This is the **smallest number** that each of the denominators will divide into evenly. The least common multiple of the denominators becomes the new denominator in both fractions. Then, for each fraction multiply the numerator by the same number you had to multiply its original denominator by to get the new denominator. For example, $\frac{3}{4} = \frac{3 \times 3}{4 \times 3} = \frac{9}{12}$.

Answer: Choice **A** is correct.

$\frac{3}{4} > \frac{1}{2}$ is true. The fraction $\frac{3}{4}$ is larger than $\frac{1}{2}$ since $\frac{3}{4} > \frac{2}{4}$.

10. Which of the following fractions is **equivalent** to $\frac{1}{2}$?

    (A) $\frac{3}{4}$

    (B) $\frac{4}{5}$

    (C) $\frac{7}{12}$

    (D) $\frac{11}{22}$

Hint #1:

Reduce each fraction to its simplest form and see which is $\frac{1}{2}$.

Hint #2:

Another way to solve this problem would be to change each of the fractions to **decimal form** by dividing each numerator by its denominator, and see which one is **equivalent** to $\frac{1}{2}$.

Answer: Choice **D** is correct.

$\frac{11}{22}$ is equal to $\frac{1}{2}$ because $\frac{1 \times 11}{2 \times 11} = \frac{11}{22}$. The simplest form of the fraction $\frac{11}{22}$ is $\frac{1}{2}$. In addition, the fraction $\frac{1}{2} = 0.5$ and $\frac{11}{22} = 11 \div 22 = 0.5$. $\frac{1}{2}$ and $\frac{11}{22}$ have the same decimal form, so they are **equivalent**.

11. Tommy is labeling a number line with the fractions below.

$$\frac{1}{2} \qquad \frac{1}{4} \qquad \frac{1}{3} \qquad \frac{3}{4}$$

When placed in order from **smallest to largest**, which is the correct order?

Write the fractions in correct order on the line below.

_____

Hint #1:

One way to compare fractions is to change each to a common denominator and compare the numerators.

Hint #2:

After they have the same denominators, look at their numerators: the larger the numerator, the larger the fraction.

Answer: The correct order from smallest to largest is $\frac{1}{4}$, $\frac{1}{3}$, $\frac{1}{2}$, and $\frac{3}{4}$.
Taking the fractions in their original order and changing to a common denominator of 12, the fractions become $\frac{6}{12}$, $\frac{3}{12}$, $\frac{4}{12}$, and $\frac{9}{12}$.

Compare the numerators of these new fractions. The smallest fraction will now have the smallest numerator. Therefore, the order of the fractions from smallest to largest is $\frac{3}{12}$, $\frac{4}{12}$, $\frac{6}{12}$, and $\frac{9}{12}$, which is equal to $\frac{1}{4}$, $\frac{1}{3}$, $\frac{1}{2}$, and $\frac{3}{4}$.

12. The **ratio** of birds to mammals at a zoo is **12 to** 4.
Which of the following also expresses this ratio?

Ⓐ 4 to 1

Ⓑ 1 to 4

Ⓒ 3 to 1

Ⓓ 1 to 3

Hint #1:

Comparing ratios is similar to comparing fractions. See if there is a **common factor** of **12** and **4**, and then divide.

Hint #2:

Be sure to keep the order of the items being compared in the ratio the same: write the number for birds **first** and the number for mammals **second**.

Answer: Choice **C** is correct.

Because the greatest common factor of 12 and 4 is **4**, divide 12 by 4 and 4 by 4 to get the values for an equivalent ratio.

12 ÷ 4 = 3 and 4 ÷ 4 = 1 to form the ratio **3 to 1.**

13. Charlie measured a **sunflower** he is growing. It is one and four tenths meters tall.

Which of the following is **equal** to the height of the flower?

(A) 14 meters

(B) 1.4 meters

(C) 1.04 meters

(D) 1.004 meters

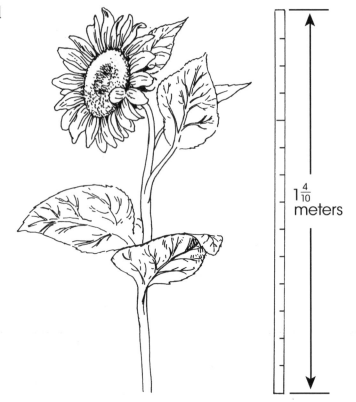

$1\frac{4}{10}$
meters

Hint #1:

Place the decimal point **after** the units place in the number.

Hint #2:

The number **1** should be to the **left** of the decimal point. The number **4** should be on the **right** side of the decimal point and located in the **tenths place**.

Answer: Choice **B** is correct.

The height of the flower is equal to **1.4 meters**. Using the information in the hints, **1** should be placed to the **left** of the decimal and **4** to the **right** of the decimal. The **tenths place** is the first place to the **right** of the decimal point. **One and four tenths** is equal to **1.4**.

14. Place the following decimals in order from **greatest** to **least** on the line below.

0.0310   0.3100   3.1000   0.0031

_____

Hint #1:

The key to solving this question is to **compare** the place values of the digits in each number. Start from the **ones place** (to the left of the decimal point) and move to the right to compare.

Hint #2:

Another way to compare decimals is to line them up one above the other to compare. When doing this, be sure to line up the decimal points.

Answer: The correct order from greatest to least is **3.1000**, **0.3100**, **0.0310**, and **0.0031**. As stated in the hints, you can compare the decimals by lining up the decimal points:

        0.0310
        0.3100
        3.1000
        0.0031

After this is done correctly, compare the numbers. The number **3.1000** would be the largest, **0.3100** the second largest, **0.0310** the third largest and **0.0031** the smallest.

15. Fill in the blank below, using **<**, **>**, or **=** to compare the following numbers:

8.908 _____ 8.9008

Hint #1:

When comparing decimals, use **place value**. Start from the left and work to the right. Look for the greatest place value where the numbers are different. Then compare these numbers to decide which symbol should be placed in the box.

Hint #2:

Looking from left to right, each of the numbers is the same until the third place to the right of the decimal point. This is the **thousandths place**.

Answer: 8.908 > 8.9008.

The decimal **8.908** is **greater** than the decimal **8.9008** because an **8** in the thousandths place is **greater** than a **0** in the thousandths place.

8.908
8.9008

16. Which of the following is **not** equivalent to 25%?

Ⓐ $\frac{25}{100}$

Ⓑ $\frac{1}{4}$

Ⓒ 0.25

Ⓓ $\frac{4}{20}$

Hint #1:

Think about different forms of numbers, such as **percents**, **fractions**, and **decimals**. Change **25%** to these different forms. See which of the numbers above does **not** match one of these forms.

Hint #2:

25% means **25 per 100**.

Answer: Choice **D** is correct.

$\frac{4}{20}$ is **not** equivalent to 25%. $\frac{4}{20} = \frac{20}{100} = 20\%$.

17. There are a total of **125 students** in the school chorus. Of these students, **62** are boys.

Written as a fraction, what is the **ratio** of boys to total students in the chorus? Write your answer on the line below.

_____

Hint #1:

A **ratio** is **a comparison of two numbers**. The two numbers that need to be compared in this ratio are the number of boys and the total number of students in the chorus.

Hint #2:

The number of boys is **62**. The total number of students is **125**. Write the ratio as a fraction using these two numbers.

Answer: The correct answer is $\frac{62}{125}$.

The number of boys is **62** and the total number of students is **125**. Be sure to write the number of boys as the numerator, or top number in the fraction, and the total number of students as the denominator.

18. In the number 5,236,109 what is the **value** of the number 3?

_____

Hint #1:

To answer this question, find the place value of the number **3**, which is five places to the **left** of where the decimal point would go. Then, multiply this place value by 3.

Hint #2:

Start at the place where the **9** is located. This is the ones place. Moving to the left are the tens place, hundreds place, thousands place, and ten thousands place. The **3** is in the ten thousands place.

Answer: In the number **5,236,109** the value of the number 3 is **30,000**. Since the 3 is located in the **ten thousands place**, multiply 3 by 10,000 to get **30,000**.

19. Tim's desk measures $2\frac{1}{2}$ **feet long.** How long is his desk in inches?

_____

Hint #1:

Use the fact that **1 foot = 12 inches** to solve the problem. Multiply the length of the desk in feet by the number of inches in a foot.

Hint #2:

Tim's desk is $2\frac{1}{2}$ feet long, which can also be written as 2.5 feet. Multiply this by 12 inches to convert the measurement to inches.

Answer: The correct answer is **30 inches**.

$2\frac{1}{2}$ **feet × 12 inches = 30 inches** or **2.5 × 12 = 30.**
Or: **2 feet × 12 inches = 24 inches.** $\frac{1}{2}$ **foot × 12 inches = 6 inches.**
24 inches + 6 inches = 30 inches.

Challenge Activity

You're doing a great job so far!
Are you ready for a Challenge Activity?

Good luck!

a) First, convert each of the following fractions so that each has the **same denominator**.

$$\frac{1}{4} \qquad \frac{5}{6} \qquad \frac{3}{4} \qquad \frac{1}{2}$$

_____

b) Next, match each of the fractions from part **a** with the letter that **best** shows its location on the number line below. Write the value in the box under the correct letter.

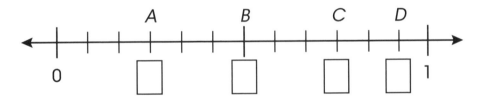

c) In the figure below, how many **squares** should be shaded so that the shaded area is equivalent to $\frac{1}{4}$ of the area of the rectangle?

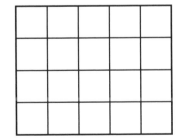

See hints and answers on following page.

Hint #1:

To find a **common denominator** in part **a**, find the least common multiple of **2, 4,** and **6**.

Hint #2:

To shade $\frac{1}{4}$ of the area in part **c**, find $\frac{1}{4}$ of the total number of squares.

Answers to Challenge Activity:

a) $\frac{1}{4} = \frac{3}{12}, \frac{5}{6} = \frac{10}{12}, \frac{3}{4} = \frac{9}{12}$, and $\frac{1}{2} = \frac{6}{12}$

To change to a common denominator, first find the least common multiple of 2, 4, and 6. This number is 12. Then change each fraction to a denominator of 12. The result is $\frac{1 \times 3}{4 \times 3} = \frac{3}{12}, \frac{5 \times 2}{6 \times 2} = \frac{3}{12}, \frac{3 \times 3}{4 \times 3} = \frac{3}{12}$, and $\frac{1 \times 6}{2 \times 6} = \frac{6}{12}$

b) Your number line should look like this:

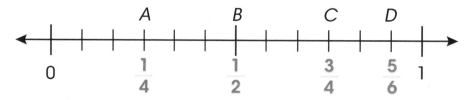

Each fraction is given a common denominator. Now, the fractions can be compared by using the numerators. The number line is divided into twelve parts. Use the value in the numerator and count over that number of spaces to find the location of each fraction.

c) The correct answer for part **c** is that any **5** of the 20 squares should be shaded. This is true because $\frac{1}{4} = \frac{1 \times 5}{4 \times 5} = \frac{5}{20}$.

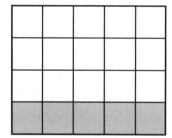

Test

Let's take a quick test and see how much you've learned during this climb up *SCORE!* Mountain.

Good luck!

1. What is the least common denominator of the fractions $\frac{6}{7}$ and $\frac{3}{5}$?

   _____

2. Which of the following is not equivalent to $\frac{3}{4}$?

   (A) $\frac{75}{100}$

   (B) 75%

   (C) $\frac{6}{8}$

   (D) 34%

3. Jason, Shelby, and Rich each ate cookies from the same jar for a snack.

   Jason ate 30% of the cookies.

   Shelby ate $\frac{1}{4}$ of the cookies.

   Rich ate $\frac{2}{5}$ of the cookies.

   Who ate the **most** cookies?

   _____

4. Elsa says that the number **16** has **four factors**.
Mike says that it has **five factors**.

Who is correct?

_____

5. Which symbol should be placed in the answer
box to make the statement **true**?

60.019 $\boxed{?}$ 60.109

_____

Answers to test questions:

1. The correct answer is **35**.

To find the least common denominator, find the smallest multiple that 7 and 5 have in common. You can do this by listing the multiples of each:
Multiples of 7 = 7, 14, 21, 28, **35**, 42, 49…
Multiples of 5 = 5, 10, 15, 20, 25, 30, **35**, 40…
The smallest number that is common to both lists is 35, the least common denominator of the fractions.

2. Choice **D** is correct.

$$34\% = \frac{34 \div 2}{100 \div 2} = \frac{17}{50}.$$

3. **Rich** ate the most cookies.

To compare the numbers, change them to the same form. One way to do this is to convert each to fraction form with a common denominator. Try a common denominator of 100.

$$30\% = \frac{30}{100} \cdot \frac{1 \times 25}{4 \times 25} = \frac{25}{100} \cdot \frac{2 \times 20}{5 \times 20} = \frac{40}{100}.$$

After changing to a denominator of 100, the largest number is $\frac{40}{100} = \frac{2}{5}$. This is the amount that **Rich** ate.

4. The total number of factors is **five**, so **Mike** is correct. The factors of a number are the whole numbers that will divide into that number without leaving a remainder. The factors of 16 are **1, 2, 4, 8,** and **16**. This is a total of **five factors**.

5. The correct answer is **<**, because **60.019** is **less** than **60.109**. When comparing decimals, work from left to right. Look for the place value where the numbers are different. Since each number has a value of 60 to the left of the decimal point, look to the right of the decimal to compare. The first number has a value of .**019**, or "**nineteen thousandths.**" The second number has a value of .**109**, or "**one hundred nine thousandths.**" The second number is larger than the first. Therefore, the answer should state that the first number is **less than** the second, so a **less than** symbol is used.

Celebrate!

Let's take a fun break before we climb up to the next base camp. You've earned it!

Let's take a break and make this delicious and healthy snack!

Ants on a log

- First, cut up some celery sticks. Ask an adult for help with cutting!

- Then, spread your favorite peanut butter onto the celery sticks.

- Finally, cover the celery sticks with raisins, just like ants on a log!

- Enjoy your snack! Share with friends or family members if you'd like!

Congratulations!
You're on your way up *SCORE!* Mountain.

BASE CAMP 1

Good luck and have fun!

You deserve it for working so hard!

Base Camp

2

Number Operations

Let's continue the climb up *SCORE!* Mountain. Are you ready? Let's get started! Good luck!

SCORE! MOUNTAIN TOP

BASE CAMP 5

BASE CAMP 4

BASE CAMP 3

BASE CAMP 2

BASE CAMP 1

1. Each row in the school auditorium has **36 seats**. There are a total of **21 rows**. How many total seats are in the auditorium? Write your answer on the line below.

_____

Hint #1:

Take the information in the question and figure out what **operation** should be performed. If the number of seats in each row and the total number of rows is given, what should be done to these two values to find the total number of seats?

Hint #2:

Take the total number of seats in each row and **multiply** it by the total number of rows in the auditorium.

Answer: The correct answer is **756 seats**.

$$
\begin{array}{r}
36 \text{ seats} \\
\times\ 21 \text{ rows} \\
\hline
\textbf{756 seats total}
\end{array}
$$

2. Shira has $10\frac{3}{4}$ **yards** of fabric. If she uses $6\frac{1}{4}$ **yards** on a project, how much fabric does she have left? Write your answer on the line below.

_____

Hint #1:

Because Shira starts with $10\frac{3}{4}$ yards and uses $6\frac{1}{4}$ yards, **subtract** these two mixed numbers to find the amount of fabric she has left over.

Hint #2:

$$10\frac{3}{4}$$
$$-\ 6\frac{1}{4}$$
$$\overline{}$$

Answer: The correct answer is $4\frac{2}{4}$ or $4\frac{1}{2}$ yards.

There is already a common denominator, so subtract the numerators and keep the denominator of 4. Then, subtract the whole numbers to get the final answer.

$$10\frac{3}{4} - 6\frac{1}{4} = 4\frac{2}{4}\text{ or }4\frac{1}{2}.$$

3. Louis has **$132** to spend on a 3-day-long trip. If he spends the **same** amount of money each day, how much will he spend on each day of the trip? Write your answer on the line below.

_____

Hint #1:

Figure out what operation should be used. If he has a total of $132 for 3 days, what operation will split that amount into 3 equal parts?

Hint #2:

The operation needed is **division**. Take the total amount he has to spend and divide it by the number of days. This gives the amount he will spend on one of the days.

Answer: The correct answer is **$44**.

$132 ÷ 3 days = $44 he will spend each day.

4. Kendal has a collection of **240 stickers**. If she places 15 stickers on each page in her album, how many pages will she need for her collection? Write your answer on the line below.

_____

Hint #1:

In order to solve this problem, figure out what **mathematical operation** should be used. If 240 stickers will be grouped into 15 stickers per page, what operation should be used?

Hint #2:

Kendal needs to **divide** her collection of 240 stickers. She will only place 15 stickers on each page. Therefore, divide 240 by 15 to find the number of pages.

Answer: Kendal will need **16 pages** for her sticker collection.

240 ÷ 15 = 16 pages.

5. On **Monday**, Toby completed $\frac{3}{8}$ of his school project. On **Tuesday**, he completed $\frac{2}{8}$ of the same project. After these two days, what **fraction** of the project has he completed? Write your answer on the line below.

_____

Hint #1:

You are trying to figure out the total amount he has completed. **Add** the amounts completed to find the total.

Hint #2:

To solve this question, you will need to **add** $\frac{3}{8}$ and $\frac{2}{8}$. There is already a common denominator, so just add the numerators and keep the denominator of 8.

Answer: After two days, Toby has completed $\frac{5}{8}$ of the project.
$$\frac{3}{8} + \frac{2}{8} = \frac{5}{8}$$

6. After starting her homework at school, Sheryl still needed to finish $\frac{5}{6}$ of her homework. She then completed $\frac{3}{6}$ of her homework after school. What **fraction** of her homework does she still need to do? Write your answer on the line below.

_____

Hint #1:

This question is looking for the amount of homework she still needs to do. Take the total amount she needed to finish and **subtract** the amount she completed after school. The answer is the amount she still needs to complete.

Hint #2:

To answer this question, subtract $\frac{3}{6}$ from $\frac{5}{6}$. There is already a common denominator, so just **subtract** the numerators and keep the denominator of 6.

Answer: Sheryl still needs to do $\frac{2}{6}$ or $\frac{1}{3}$ of her homework.
$\frac{5}{6} - \frac{3}{6} = \frac{2}{6}$, which simplifies to $\frac{1}{3}$.

7. Tickets to the movies cost $6.75 each. If Jo Ann and 3 of her friends are going, **estimate** the total amount they will spend on the tickets. Write your answer on the line below.

_____

Hint #1:

In order to estimate the total amount, **round** the cost of a ticket to the nearest dollar.

Hint #2:

Remember, Jo Ann is going with 3 of her friends. That means 4 tickets are needed!

Answer: The estimated cost is **$28**.

The ticket price of $6.75 is close to $7.00. To find the total amount the four friends will spend, multiply 7 and 4.

The result is **$7 × 4 = $28**.

8. In the school drama club, there are **157 students**.
What is this number rounded to the **nearest ten**?

_____

Hint #1:

Remember, to **round a number**, find the digit one space to the right of the place value you are rounding to. If this digit is **5** or greater, round up. If this digit is less than **5**, keep the digit the same. In both cases, change the digits to the right of the place being rounded to zeros.

Hint #2:

In the number **157**, the digit in the tens place is **5**. The digit directly to the right of this place value is **7**.

Answer: 157 rounded to the nearest ten is **160**.

As stated in the hint, the number **157** has the digit **5** in the **tens place**. The digit directly to the right of this place is **7**. Because **7** is greater than **5**, round the digit in the tens place up, from **5** to **6**. Then place a zero in the ones place to get a final answer of **160**.

9. Find the **sum** of the following numbers.

$$1.325 + 6.47$$

Write your answer on the line below.

_____

Hint #1:

In order to **add decimals**, first line up the decimal points. Then add the numbers. Place the decimal point in the answer directly below the decimal points in the addends.

Hint #2:

After lining up the decimal points, the problem should look like this:

$$\begin{array}{r} 1.325 \\ + \ 6.47 \\ \hline \end{array}$$

Answer: The correct answer is **7.795**.

As stated in the hints above, add the decimals with the decimal points lined up. Place the decimal point in the answer directly below the decimal points in the addends.

$$\begin{array}{r} 1.325 \\ + \ 6.47 \\ \hline 7.795 \end{array}$$

10. Multiply the following numbers.

6.23 and 4.5

Write your answer on the line below.

_____

Hint #1:

To **multiply decimals**, multiply the numbers as you would multiply whole numbers. Then, count the total number of decimal places in the original decimal numbers being multiplied. This total number of decimal places determines where to place the decimal point in the answer.

Hint #2:

To find the answer, multiply **623** by **45**. Then, count the number of decimal places in the original decimal numbers to be multiplied. In the product, start at the rightmost digit and count to the left the number of places to put the decimal point in the final answer.

Answer: The correct answer is **28.035**.

First multiply **623** and **45** to get **28035**. Count the number of decimal places in each of the original decimal numbers.

6.23	In **6.23**, there are **2 decimal places**.
× 4.5	In **4.5**, there is **1**.
28.035	This is a total of **3 decimal places**.

Take the answer to **623 × 45** and place the decimal point **3** places over from the right: **28035** becomes **28.035**.

11. Becky made $2\frac{1}{2}$ **dozen** cookies.

Stanley made $3\frac{2}{5}$ **dozen** cookies.

How many dozen cookies did Becky and Stanley make **together**?
Write your answer on the line below.

_____

Hint #1:

This question is looking for the **total amount**. Add the mixed numbers in the problem to find the total.

Hint #2:

To add the **mixed numbers**, first add the fractions. There is already a common denominator, so add the numerators and keep the denominator of 5. Then add the whole numbers.

Answer: Becky and Stanley made a total of $5\frac{3}{5}$ **dozen cookies**.

To get the answer, find the sum of the two amounts.

$$2\frac{1}{5}$$
$$+\ 3\frac{2}{5}$$
$$\overline{5\frac{3}{5}}$$

2. The school record for the 100-meter dash is **13.628 seconds**.
What is this record rounded to the nearest **hundredth**?
Write your answer on the line below.

_____

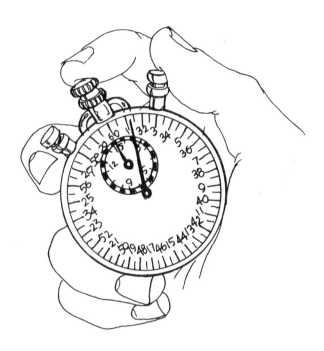

Hint #1:

To **round** a number, find the digit one place to the right of the place value you are rounding to. If this digit is 5 or greater, **round up**. If this digit is less than 5, **keep the digit the same**. In both cases, drop the digits to the **right** of the place you are rounding to.

Hint #2:

In the number **13.628**, the digit **2** is in the **hundredths place**.

Answer: The correct answer is **13.63 seconds**.

Since the digit **2** is in the **hundredths place**, look one place to the right. The digit in this place is **8**. Since **8** is greater than **5**, round the **2** in the hundredths up to **3**. Then, drop the digit **8** to the right of this place. This gives an answer of **13.63**.

13. Evaluate the following expression:

$$16 - 4 \times 3 \div 2$$

Write your answer on the line below.

_____

Hint #1:

This question needs to be simplified using the order of operations. This order can be remembered with **PEMDAS**: **P**arentheses, **E**xponents, **M**ultiply and **D**ivide, **A**dd and **S**ubtract.

Hint #2:

There are no parentheses or exponents, so the first operation that should be performed is **multiplication**.

Answer: The correct answer is **10**.

Start by multiplying: **4 × 3 = 12**.
The expression then becomes **16 − 12 ÷ 2**. Next, divide **12** by **2**.
The expression becomes **16 − 6**.
Now, subtract to get the final answer of **10**.

14. Evaluate the following expression:

$$(10 + 6) - (3 \times 5)$$

Write your answer on the line below.

_____

Hint #1:

This question needs to be simplified using the order of operations. Remember, the order is **PEMDAS**: **P**arentheses, **E**xponents, **M**ultiply and **D**ivide, **A**dd and **S**ubtract.

Hint #2:

There are parentheses in the question. Do the operations within the parentheses **first**. In the first set of parentheses, add **10** and **6**. In the second set of parentheses, multiply **3** and **5**. To complete the problem, subtract these two results.

Answer: The correct answer is **1**.

Evaluate inside the parentheses first to get **16 − 15**.
Then subtract: **16 − 15 = 1**.

15. **Evaluate** the following expression:

2.55 ÷ 1.7

Write your answer on the line below.

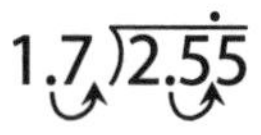

_____

© Kaplan Publishing, Inc.

16. When evaluating the expression $21 \div 3 - 4 \times 1$, which operation should be performed **first**?

(A) multiplication

(B) division

(C) subtraction

(D) parentheses

Hint #1:

This question can be answered by using the correct order of operations. This order can be remembered with **PEMDAS**.

Hint #2:

What is the first operation in **PEMDAS** that appears in the expression above?

Answer: Choice **B** is correct.

There are no parentheses or exponents. Do multiplication and division in order from left to right. The **division** is the first operation on the left. In evaluating this expression the first step would be **21 ÷ 3**.

17. Penny has $10\frac{1}{3}$ **feet** of railing on her new deck. What is this amount written as an **improper fraction**?

_____

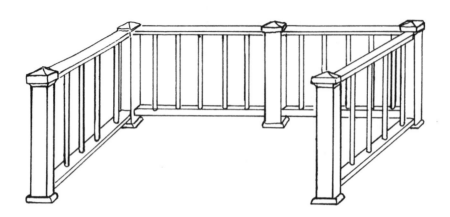

Hint #1:

An **improper fraction** has a numerator that is greater than or equal to its denominator.

Hint #2:

To change a **mixed number** to an **improper fraction**, first multiply the whole number by the denominator. Then add this amount to the numerator. This result should be placed over the denominator to form the improper fraction.

Answer: The correct answer is $\frac{31}{3}$.

First, multiply: **10 × 3 = 30**.
Then, add: **30 + 1 = 31**.
Place this new numerator over 3 to get the improper fraction $\frac{31}{3}$.

18. Write the following improper fraction as a **mixed number**: $\frac{11}{4}$.

_____

Hint #1:

To change an **improper fraction** to a **mixed number**, find the number of times that the denominator divides into the numerator. This becomes the whole number part of the mixed number.

Hint #2:

Next, place the remainder over the denominator. This becomes the fractional part of the mixed number.

Answer: The correct answer is $2\frac{3}{4}$.

11 ÷ 4 = 2 with a remainder of **3**. Therefore, the **2** becomes the whole number part of the mixed number. The **3** becomes the numerator of the fractional part of the mixed number. This gives an answer of $2\frac{3}{4}$.

19. Zoe, a student at Brookville Elementary School, is trying to determine the weight of each of her shoes. Which of the following is the most reasonable estimate for the weight of each of Zoe's shoes?

Ⓐ 12 ounces

Ⓑ 12 pounds

Ⓒ 12 liters

Ⓓ 12 meters

Hint #1:

Make sure that the label is a unit that is used for measuring the **weight** of something, **not** the volume or length.

Hint #2:

To make sure that the estimate is reasonable, think about the **unit label** and something that may weigh that amount. For example, if a small dog weighs 12 pounds, would Zoe's shoe weigh about the same as a dog?

Answer: Choice **A** is correct.

A shoe could weigh about **12 ounces**. Choice **B**, 12 pounds, would be too heavy for a shoe. In choices **C** and **D**, the units are not used to measure the weight of something. Liters are used to measure volume, and meters are used to measure length.

Challenge Activity

You're doing a great job so far!
Are you ready for a Challenge Activity?

Good luck!

Toby and Sam are going on a trip. Their car gets **22 miles per gallon** of gas. They will travel to their destination and then return back home.

a) If the trip is **253 miles** one way, how many total miles will they travel?

_____

b) How many gallons of gas will they use for their round-trip?

_____

c) If gas costs **$2.95 per gallon**, how much money will they spend on gas for their entire trip?

_____

See hints and answers on following page.

Hint #1:

To find how many gallons of gas they will use, **divide** the total number of miles they will drive by the number of miles per gallon the car gets.

Hint #2:

To find the amount of money they will spend on gas, use the number of gallons they used for their round-trip. Then, **multiply** this amount by the average price per gallon.

Answers to Challenge Activity:

a) If the trip is **253 miles** one way, they will travel a total of **506 miles**.

Toby and Sam are traveling to their destination and back. This is a total of 253 miles there and 253 miles back home.
253 + 253 = 506 miles for the entire trip.

b) Toby and Sam will use **23 gallons of gas** for their round-trip.

To find the total gallons used, divide the total miles by the number of miles per gallon. **506 miles ÷ 22 miles per gallon = 23 gallons**

c) Toby and Sam will spend **$67.85** on gas for their entire trip.

To find the amount spent on gas, take the number of gallons used and multiply by the price per gallon.
23 gallons × $2.95 per gallon = $67.85

Test

Let's take a quick test and see how much you've learned during this climb up *SCORE!* Mountain.

Good luck!

1. In the gymnasium, the students are asked to line up in 12 rows. If there are 16 students in a row, how many students have lined up?

   _____

2. Evaluate the expression: $100 \div 10 - 5 \times 2$

   _____

3. What is the value of the fraction $\frac{12}{32}$ in lowest terms?

   _____

4. Shari ran the first leg of a relay race in 40.82 seconds. Kathleen ran the second leg in 37.5 seconds. What was their total time, in seconds, for both legs of the race?

_____

5. The school store sold 122 pencils and 34 erasers in one day. Each pencil cost $0.25 and each eraser cost $0.10. Which is the best estimate for the amount of money spent at the school store that day?

Ⓐ $3.40

Ⓑ $33.00

Ⓒ $45.00

Ⓓ $300.00

Answers to test questions:

1. The correct answer is **192 students**.

To find the total number of students, multiply 12 rows by 16 students per row. $12 \times 16 = $ **192 students**.

2. The correct answer is **0**.

This question needs to be simplified using the order of operations. This order can be remembered with the word **PEMDAS**: **P**arentheses, **E**xponents, **M**ultiply and **D**ivide, **A**dd and **S**ubtract. Since the expression does not contain parentheses or exponents, divide and multiply in order from left to right.

$100 \div 10 = 10$ **and** $5 \times 2 = 10$

To complete the problem, subtract these results: $10 - 10 = 0$.

3. The correct answer is $\frac{3}{8}$.

To simplify the fraction, find the greatest common factor of **12** and **32**. The largest number that will evenly divide into both 12 and 32 is **4**. Now, divide numerator and denominator by the common factor of 4: $\frac{12 \div 4}{32 \div 4} = \frac{3}{8}$.

4. The correct answer is **78.32 seconds**.

To find the total time, add the two decimals. Be sure to line up the decimal points.

$$
\begin{array}{r}
40.82 \\
+ \ 37.5 \ \\
\hline
78.32
\end{array}
$$

5. The correct answer is choice **B**.

Round **122** to **120** and then multiply **120** by **$0.25** to get **$30.00**. This is the estimated amount of money spent on pencils. Then multiply **30** by **$0.10** to get **$3.00** to find the money spent on erasers. Add these two amounts to get the estimate: **$30.00 + $3.00 = $33.00**.

Celebrate!

Let's take a fun break before we go to the next base camp. You've earned it!

Get out a deck of cards and let's have some fun!

Challenge a friend or family member to a fun game of **Memory**.

Rules of Memory

- One player shuffles the cards and places them all face down on a table. Make sure that you play on a big enough space to put all the cards down flat!

- The first player chooses two cards and turns them over, searching for a **pair**. A pair is a set of two cards with the same number; the suit doesn't matter.

Congratulations!
You're getting closer to the top of *SCORE!* Mountain.

- If the two cards chosen form a **pair**, then the player collects the cards in his or her pile and chooses two more cards.

- The player keeps going until two cards that are **not** a pair are chosen. These cards are flipped over and returned to their original locations on the table and the next player gets to choose.

- The game continues until all the cards are collected.

- The player who collects the most card pairs is the winner!

If you like, you can also make a **house of cards**! Take turns with a friend or family member to see who can make the **tallest** house of cards before it collapses!

Good luck and have fun!
You deserve it for working so hard!

Base Camp

3

Geometry and Measurement

Are you ready for another fun climb up *SCORE!* Mountain? Let's get started! Good luck!

SCORE! MOUNTAIN TOP

BASE CAMP 5

BASE CAMP 4

BASE CAMP 3

BASE CAMP 2

BASE CAMP 1

1. The figure below shows the shape of Ella's play area in meters (m).

What is the **perimeter** of this shape?

_____

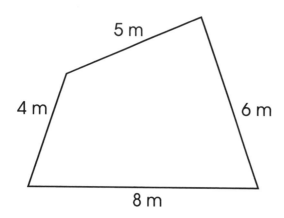

5 m

4 m

6 m

8 m

Hint #1:

The **perimeter** of a figure is the distance around the figure.

Hint #2:

This figure is a **quadrilateral** so it has four sides. Use the formula **Perimeter = side + side + side + side** to calculate the perimeter of the object.

Answer: The perimeter of Ella's play area is **23 m**.

The perimeter is found by adding up the lengths of the sides of the figure. Add each of the sides of the quadrilateral: **4 + 5 + 6 + 8 = 23 m**.

© Kaplan Publishing, Inc.

2. If two angles of a triangle are 53 and 48 degrees, what is the measure of the **third angle**?

_____

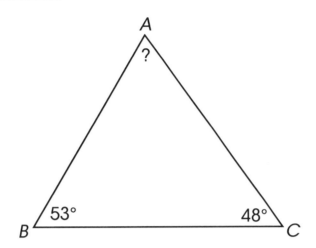

Hint #1:

The sum of the measures of the interior angles of any triangle is always **180 degrees**.

Hint #2:

Find the total number of degrees of the two given angles and **subtract** this number from 180.

Answer: The correct answer is **79 degrees**.

The known angles of **53 degrees** and **48 degrees** add up to **101 degrees**. Subtract **101** from **180** to find the measure of the third angle. **180 − 101 = 79 degrees**.

3. Fill in the blank.

The figure below can best be classified as a _____ .

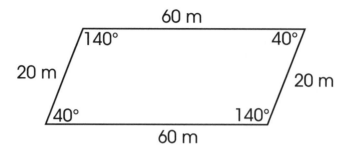

Hint #1:

Geometric figures are classified, or named, according to the **number of sides** and the **type of angles** they contain. Start by counting the number of sides in the figure and looking for any special types of angles.

Hint #2:

The figure above has **four sides** and each pair of opposite sides is **congruent** (the same length) and **parallel**.

Answer: The figure can best be classified as a **parallelogram**.

A **parallelogram** is a four-sided figure with opposite sides that are parallel and congruent.

4. The triangles below are similar. What is the **ratio** between the lengths of their corresponding sides? The ratio should be expressed with the smaller number first.

_____

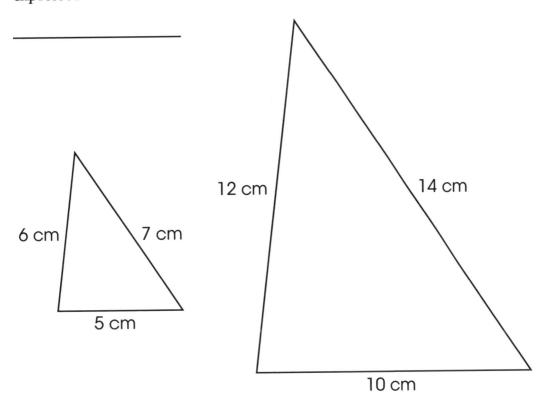

12 cm

14 cm

6 cm

7 cm

5 cm

10 cm

Hint #1:

Similar triangles are the same shape, just different sizes.

Hint #2:

Look for a number that can be multiplied by each of the sides of the smaller triangle to give the measure of each of the sides of the larger triangle.

Answer: The ratio is **1 to 2** or **1:2**.

The side that measures **5 cm** in the smaller triangle corresponds to the side that measures **10 cm** in the larger triangle.

Since $\frac{10}{5} = 2$, this side is **two times**, or twice, as long. Each of the other pairs of sides will follow this pattern. Since each of the sides of the larger triangle is two times longer than the corresponding side of the smaller triangle, the ratio is **1 to 2** or **1:2**.

5. Katie arrives at school each day at **8:30** A.M. She leaves school at **3:25** P.M. How long is she at school each day?

_____

Hint #1:

First try to **estimate** by figuring out the elapsed time if she were to leave at 3:30 P.M., instead of 3:25 P.M.

Hint #2:

Count the hours from 8:30 A.M. to 3:30 P.M. Take this elapsed time and **subtract** 5 minutes to find the actual length of time she is at school each day.

Answer: The correct answer is **6 hours, 55 minutes**.

By using the hints above, you'll find that **7 hours** elapse from 8:30 A.M. to 3:30 P.M. Subtracting **5 minutes** from 7 hours results in an elapsed time of **6 hours, 55 minutes**.

6. The triangles shown below are similar. What side of **triangle DEF** corresponds to side $\overline{AB}$ in **triangle ABC**?

_____

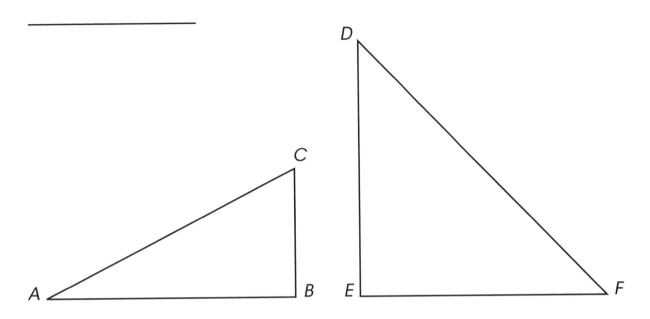

Hint #1:

Parts of objects that **correspond** are parts that would match up if one figure were placed on top of the other.

Hint #2:

It might be helpful to **trace** triangle ABC. Slide this copy of triangle *ABC* onto triangle *DEF* so that the triangles have the same orientation (for example, smallest angles to the left). Find side $\overline{AB}$ and locate the side from triangle *DEF* that corresponds to (matches up with) this side.

Answer: The correct answer is side $\overline{DE}$.

When placed side by side, or one on top of the other, sides $\overline{AB}$ and $\overline{DE}$ would match up.

7. The triangle below has **two congruent sides**. It can be best classified as a(n) _____ triangle.

Ⓐ right

Ⓑ isosceles

Ⓒ scalene

Ⓓ equilateral

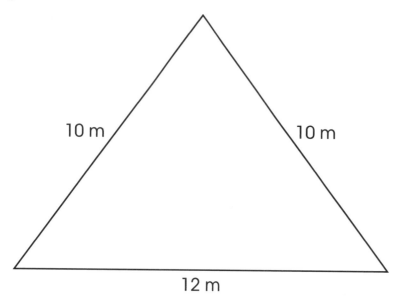

10 m   10 m

12 m

Hint #1:

The triangle has two sides that are **congruent**, or have the same length.

Hint #2:

The term **equilateral** means that all 3 sides are the same length.

Answer: Choice **B** is correct.

The word **isosceles** means that 2 of the 3 sides have the same length.

8. Which two triangles below are **congruent**?

_____

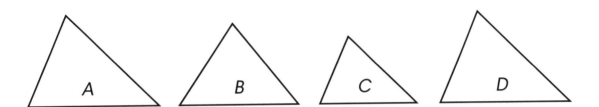

Hint #1:

Remember, the word **congruent** means that the triangles are the **same shape** and **size**.

Hint #2:

Find two figures that look identical. These are congruent triangles.

Answer: Triangles **A** and **D** are **congruent**. They have the same shape and size. Triangles **A** and **C** are **similar triangles** but not congruent triangles. They are the same shape but different sizes.

9. In **quadrilateral** *ABCD*, what is the measure of **angle *A*?**

_____

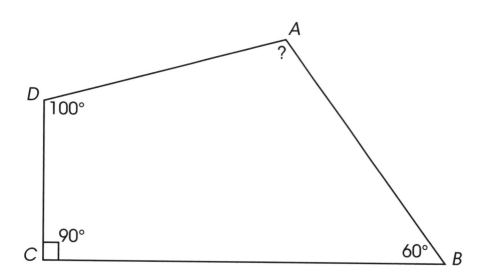

Hint #1:

The **sum** of the interior angles in any quadrilateral is **360°**.

Hint #2:

Find the **sum** of the three known angles of quadrilateral *ABCD*. Then, **subtract** this sum from 360 degrees. This will give the measure of angle *A*.

Answer: The measure of angle *A* is **110 degrees**.

The three known angles add to 250 degrees: **90° + 100° + 60° = 250°**.
360 − 250 = 110 degrees

10. The **grid** shows the location of some places in Sun City. Using **coordinates**, what is the location of the park?

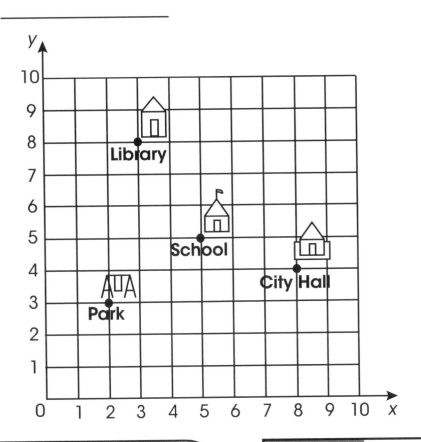

Hint #1:

When using **coordinates**, the **first number** in the pair is the **x-value**. This is the number of units to count **right** from the **origin** (0, 0). The **second number** in the pair is the **y-value**. This is the number of units to count **up** from the origin.

Hint #2:

To find the coordinates, start from the **origin** (0, 0). Count the number of units over and then up to get to the park. Use these numbers to give the location of the park.

Answer: The park is at the point **(2, 3)**.

The park is **2 units right** and **three units up** from the origin (0, 0). The **x-value** (number of units right) is always written first and the **y-value** (number of units up) is written second in the pair.

11. Plot and label the following points on the coordinate grid below.

M (1, 2), **A** (3, 2), **T** (3, 4), **H** (1, 4)

What is the **best** name for the geometric shape formed when the points in **MATH** are connected? _____

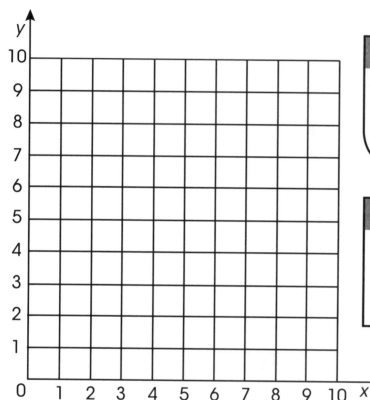

> ### Hint #1:
> Be sure to connect the points in order. Connect **M** to **A**, **A** to **T**, **T** to **H**, and **H** back to **M**.

> ### Hint #2:
> The figure formed has opposite sides that are **congruent** (same length) and **parallel**.

Answer: The graph with the points in **MATH** plotted correctly is shown at right.

The shape formed when the points are connected is a **square**. The figure has four sides where all sides are the same length and opposite sides are parallel. Each angle is a right angle so this is a **square**.

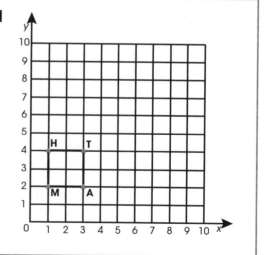

12. Draw all the different **lines of symmetry** on the triangle below. How many are there?

_____

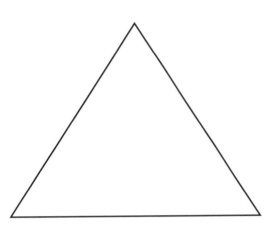

Hint #1:

A **line of symmetry** cuts a figure in **half**. The halves would match up if the figure were folded over on the line of symmetry.

Hint #2:

In this triangle, there is more than one line of symmetry.

Answer: There are **3 lines of symmetry** for the triangle. Here's what it looks like with the lines of symmetry drawn in.

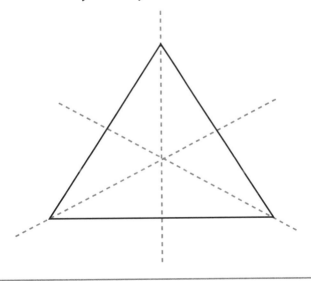

13. Measure the length of the toy car in inches.

You will need a ruler for this question.

length = _____

Hint #1:

Be sure to use the **inches** side of a ruler to measure. Make sure to start at **zero** on the ruler, and line it up with one end of the car. Then, find the line on the ruler that matches up with the other end of the car.

Hint #2:

The **longest** lines on the ruler represent the **inches**. The **shorter** lines in between the longest lines represent the parts of an inch. For example, the line halfway between 4 and 5 inches is $4\frac{1}{2}$ inches. The line halfway between 4 and $4\frac{1}{2}$ inches is $4\frac{1}{4}$ inches.

Answer: The car measures $4\frac{1}{2}$ inches.

Line up the mark for zero on one end of the car. The line halfway between 3 and 4 lines up with the other end of the car. This line represents the measurement $4\frac{1}{2}$ inches.

14. Tyler measured his room to be **3 yards** long. How many **feet long** is his room?

_____

Hint #1:

There are **3 feet** in **1 yard**.

Hint #2:

You can use this **proportion** to solve the problem:
$$\frac{3 \text{ feet}}{1 \text{ yard}} = \frac{x \text{ feet}}{3 \text{ yards}}.$$

Answer: Tyler's room is **9 feet long.**

Since there are 3 feet in 1 yard, use the proportion $\frac{3 \text{ feet}}{1 \text{ yard}} = \frac{x \text{ feet}}{3 \text{ yards}}$.

Because **1 × 3 = 3** in the denominator, solve for x by multiplying the numerator by 3. $\frac{3 \times 3}{1 \times 3} = \frac{9 \text{ feet}}{3 \text{ yards}}$. There are **9 feet** in **3 yards**.

15. Jamal is running a **5-kilometer** road race. How many **meters** long is this race?

_____

Hint #1:

There are **1,000 meters** in **1 kilometer**.

Hint #2:

You can use a **proportion** to solve the problem:
$$\frac{1{,}000 \text{ meters}}{1 \text{ kilometer}} = \frac{x \text{ meters}}{5 \text{ kilometers}}.$$

Answer: Jamal's race is **5000 meters long**.

Since there are 1,000 meters in 1 kilometer, use the proportion:
$\frac{1{,}000 \text{ meters}}{1 \text{ kilometer}} = \frac{x \text{ meters}}{5 \text{ kilometers}}$. Because **1 × 5 = 5** in the denominator, solve for **x** by also multiplying the numerator by 5. $\frac{1{,}000 \times 5}{1 \times 5} = \frac{5{,}000 \text{ meters}}{5 \text{ kilometers}}$.

There are **5,000 meters** in **5 kilometers**.

16. Joe wants to measure the **height** of his front door.
Which of the following is the **best tool** for him to use?

(A) a protractor

(B) a bathroom scale

(C) a tape measure

(D) a ruler

Hint #1:

Be sure to select a tool that measures the **length** of objects, not the weight of objects or the number of degrees in an angle.

Hint #2:

Estimate the height of Joe's door. It is most likely **taller** than an adult. Which of these tools would be best to measure a height of over **6 feet**?

Answer: Choice **C** is correct.

The best tool to measure Joe's front door would be **a tape measure**.
A **ruler** is also used to measure length, but would be much shorter than
a tape measure and not the best choice.

17. What time could it be when the hour and minute hands on a clock form a **right angle**?

Ⓐ 6:00

Ⓑ 7:00

Ⓒ 8:00

Ⓓ 9:00

Hint #1:

A **right angle** has **90 degrees** in it, and is shaped like a capital letter **L**.

Hint #2:

The hands of a clock would form a 90-degree angle when they are **three numbers apart**. Which one of the above times would have the two hands on numbers that are three apart?

© Kaplan Publishing, Inc.

Answer: Choice **D** is correct.

At **9:00**, the **minute** hand is on the **9** and the **hour** hand is on the **12**. This would form a 90-degree, or right angle.

74 SCORE! *Mountain Challenge*

18. Which of the following is the **best estimate** for the measure of the angle below?

(A) 90 degrees

(B) 120 degrees

(C) 30 degrees

(D) 180 degrees

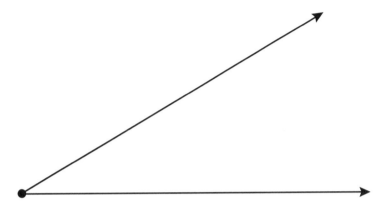

Hint #1:

This is an **acute angle**.

Hint #2:

A **right angle** measures exactly **90 degrees**.

Answer: Choice **C** is correct.

The best estimate for the measure of the angle is **30 degrees**. The angle is **acute**. This means it measures between **0** and **90 degrees**.

19. Jesse is measuring the **length** of his arm. Which unit of measurement would be the **easiest** to measure his arm with?

Ⓐ millimeters

Ⓑ grams

Ⓒ kilometers

Ⓓ inches

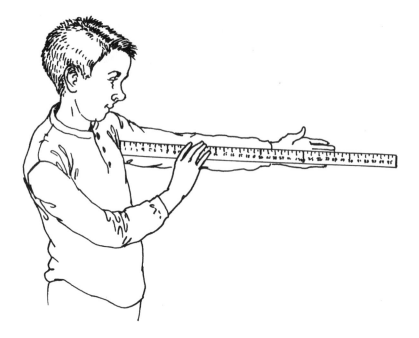

Hint #1:

Be sure to use a unit that measures the **length** of objects, not the **mass** of objects.

Hint #2:

Select a unit of length that is appropriate for the length of an arm, which is probably about 2 feet long. Some units of length may be too large or too small.

Answer: Choice **D** is correct.

The unit of measurement that would be easiest for Jesse to measure his arm with would be **inches**. A **millimeter** is a unit of length but is much too small to be an appropriate choice. A **kilometer** is also a unit of length but is much too large to measure the length of an arm. The unit **gram** is used to measure the mass of an object.

You're doing a great job so far!
Are you ready for a Challenge Activity?

Good luck!

a) Plot and label the points for each figure on the grid below. Connect the points in order to form two different geometric shapes.

Figure 1: A(1, 3); B(3, 3); C(3, 1); D(1, 1).

Figure 2: W(4, 5); X(7, 5); Y(7, 10); Z(4, 10).

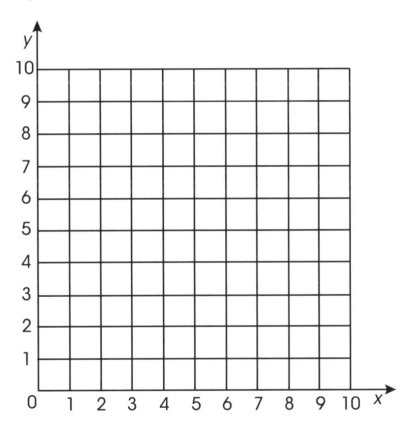

b) Find the **perimeter** of each figure from **part a**.

Perimeter of Figure 1: _____

Perimeter of Figure 2: _____

c) Of the two figures graphed on page 77, which is a **regular polygon**?

_____

Hint #1:

Remember, the **perimeter** is the distance around an object. To find the perimeter of a figure, use the formula **Perimeter = side + side + side + side**.

Hint #2:

Regular polygons have all sides of the same length and all angles of the **same measure**.

Answers to Challenge Activity:

a) In order to graph points on a grid, start at 0. Then, use the numbers in the pair. Go right the number of units in the **x-value** (first number) and up the number of units in the **y-value** (second number). Label each point with the correct letter. The grid below shows the points correctly plotted and labeled:

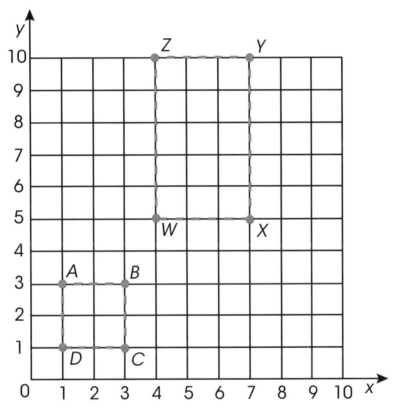

b) **Figure 1** has a perimeter of **8 units**.
   Figure 2 has a perimeter of **16 units**.

   Remember, to find the perimeter of a figure use the formula
   Perimeter = side + side + side + side.

   In **Figure 1**, each side has a length of 2 units.
   ***P* = 2 + 2 + 2 + 2 = 8 units**.
   In **Figure 2**, the length is equal to 3 units and the width is equal to 5 units.
   ***P* = 5 + 3 + 5 + 3 = 16 units**.

c) **Figure 1**, the **square**, is a **regular polygon**. Each angle of a square is **equal** to 90 degrees. Each side of a square is the **same length**. In this problem, each side of square *ABCD* is **2 units**. The rectangle is not a regular polygon because each of the sides is not the same length.

Let's take a quick test and see how much you've learned during this climb up *SCORE!* Mountain.

Good luck!

1. Jake measures his height to be 4 feet 4 inches. What would his height be if measured completely in inches?

2. Graph and label points **A**(1, 1); **B**(3, 1); **C**(4, 3); and **D**(2, 3) on the grid below. When the points are connected in order, the geometric shape *ABCD* is formed. What is the best name for this shape?

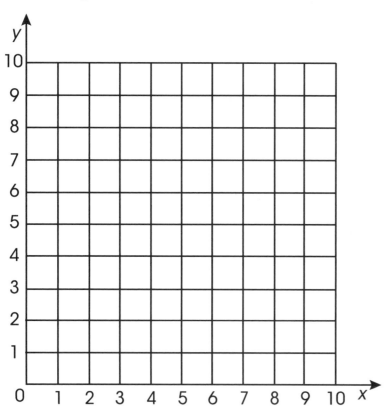

3. The figure below shows the dimensions in feet of the Smith family's living room. What is the perimeter of this room?

_____

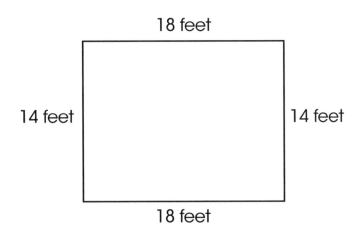

18 feet

14 feet   14 feet

18 feet

4. If two angles of a triangle are 65 degrees and 35 degrees, what is the measure of the third angle?

_____

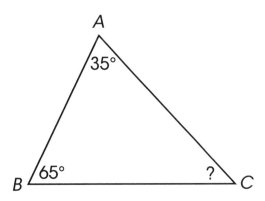

A

35°

B 65°   ? C

5. On Saturdays, the local skateboard park is open from 7:45 A.M. to 4:30 P.M. How many hours is the park open on Saturday?

_____

See answers on following page.

Answers to test questions:

1. The correct answer is **52 inches**.

Use the fact that **1 foot = 12 inches** to set up equivalent fractions:

$$\frac{1 \text{ foot}}{12 \text{ inches}} = \frac{4 \text{ feet}}{? \text{ inches}}.$$

Since **1 × 4 = 4 feet**, multiply **12 × 4** in the denominator:

$$\frac{1 \text{ foot} \times 4}{12 \text{ inches} \times 4} = \frac{4 \text{ feet}}{48 \text{ inches}}.$$

Now add the other 4 inches to get the total height: **48 + 4 = 52 inches**.

2. When each of the points is plotted and connected in the order **ABCD**, this is how it should look:

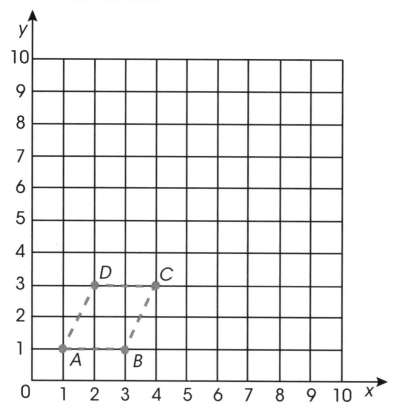

This shape is a **parallelogram**. It has opposite sides that are congruent and parallel.

Answers to test questions, *continued*:

3. The correct answer is **64 feet**.

Add the lengths of each of the sides of the room to find the perimeter. Use the perimeter formula to calculate the perimeter of the room. ***Perimeter = side + side + side + side = 14 + 18 + 14 + 18 = 64 feet.***

4. The correct answer is **80 degrees**.

The three angles of any triangle have a sum of **180 degrees**. Add the two known angles: **65 + 35 = 100**.

Subtract this total from 180 degrees to find the measure of the third angle: **180 − 100 = 80 degrees**.

5. The correct answer is **8 hours, 45 minutes**.

Use estimation skills to solve this problem. Assume that the skateboard park opens at **7:30 A.M.** instead of **7:45 A.M.** There are **9 hours** between 7:30 A.M. and 4:30 P.M. Since the park actually doesn't open until **15 minutes later**, at 7:45 A.M., subtract 15 minutes from 9 hours, which gives you **8 hours, 45 minutes**.

Celebrate!

Let's take a fun break before we go to the next base camp. You've earned it!

Congratulations!
You're halfway to the top of *SCORE!* Mountain.

Time to get on your feet and move!

Put on your favorite song and dance to the music!

It's great exercise and lots of fun!

Whatever your favorite song is, turn it on and have a good time!

Sing along with your favorite song and get moving!

Have a lip-syncing contest with your friends!

Good luck and have fun!

You deserve it for working so hard!

Base Camp

4

Algebra

Wow! You're getting close to the top of *SCORE!* Mountain. Are you ready for another fun climb? Let's get started! Good luck!

SCORE! MOUNTAIN TOP

BASE CAMP 5

BASE CAMP 4

BASE CAMP 3

BASE CAMP 2

BASE CAMP 1

1. In the equation below, which of the following is the **variable**?

$$10 \times n + 6 = 26$$

(A) 10

(B) n

(C) 6

(D) 26

Hint #1:

The **variable** in an equation is **the unknown value**.

Hint #2:

The variable is usually represented by a **circle**, **box**, **symbol**, or **letter** of the alphabet.

Answer: Choice **B** is correct.

The variable in this equation is represented by the letter **n**.

2. Brenda and Pete each simplified the expression $16 - 5 \times n + 2$, where $n = 3$.

Brenda got an answer of **3**.
Pete got an answer of **35**.

Which of these solutions is correct?
Write your answer on the line below.

_____

Hint #1:

This question needs to be simplified using the correct order of operations. This order can be remembered with the word **PEMDAS**: **P**arentheses, **E**xponents, **M**ultiply and **D**ivide, **A**dd and **S**ubtract.

Hint #2:

Since this question does not have parentheses, start by substituting **3** for *n* and multiply **5 × 3**. Then subtract and add in order from left to right.

Answer: Brenda got the correct answer of **3**.

First, substitute **3** for *n*: $16 - 5 \times 3 + 2$.
Next, multiply **5 × 3**: $16 - 15 + 2$.
Then, subtract **16 − 15**: $1 + 2$
The expression is now **1 + 2** which equals **3**.
To get an **incorrect** answer of 35, Pete performed the operations in order from left to right, instead of following the correct order of operations (**PEMDAS**).

3. Which statement means the same as "three times a number plus four"?

(A) $3 \div n + 4$

(B) $3 \times n \times 4$

(C) $3 \times n + 4$

(D) $3 + n \times 4$

Hint #1:

In this question you are asked to change a statement written in **words** to a statement written in **numbers** and **math symbols**. Look for **key words** in the statement and use those key words to determine the numbers and symbols that should be used in place of the words.

Hint #2:

The word "**times**" is a key word for multiplication. The place in the statement that states the words "**a number**" is replaced by the letter **n**. The word "**plus**" is a key word for addition. Look for the answer choice that has these symbols in the **correct order**.

Answer: Choice **C** is correct.

"**Three times a number**" should be written as **3 × n** and "**plus four**" should be written as **+ 4**.

Putting these together, the correct answer is **3 × n + 4**.

4. Find the value of y in the number sentence below.

$$6 \times y = 300$$

_____

Hint #1:

To find the number that should go in place of **y**, think to yourself, "**6 times what number gives 300 as an answer?**"

Hint #2:

Another way to solve this problem is to work **backward**. The opposite of multiplying is **dividing**. If **6** times a number is **300**, you can find **y** by dividing 300 by 6.

Answer: The correct answer is **50**.

$6 \times 50 = 300$, and $300 \div 6 = 50$.

5. Evaluate the expression below for $n = 5$.

$6 + n - 4 \div 2$

_____

Hint #1:

First, substitute **5** for the letter **n**. Then evaluate using the order of operations. Remember, this order can be remembered with the "word" **PEMDAS**: **P**arentheses, **E**xponents, **M**ultiply and **D**ivide, **A**dd and **S**ubtract.

Hint #2:

Since the expression does **not** contain parentheses or exponents, **divide** first.

Answer: The correct answer is **9**.

First, substitute **n = 5** to get **6 + 5 − 4 ÷ 2**.
Next, divide to get **6 + 5 − 2**.
Now, add and subtract in order from left to right. **6 + 5 = 11**.
11 − 2 = 9

. In the equation $n + 3 = 15$, what is the value of n?

_____

Hint #1:

To solve an equation, get the variable alone on one side. Use the inverse of addition to do this here.

Hint #2:

The inverse, or opposite, of **adding 3** is **subtracting 3**. Subtract 3 from each side of the equation to get n alone on one side.

Answer: The correct answer is **12**.

Subtract 3 from each side of the equation to get the variable alone.

$$n + 3 = 15$$
$$-3 = -3$$
$$n = 12$$

7. What is the next number in the **sequence** below?

1, 7, 13, 19, 25, _____

Hint #1:

Start with the **first** two numbers in the pattern. See what the difference is between these two numbers. Then, check to see if this is the same as the difference between the second and third numbers.

Hint #2:

The numbers are **increasing** as the pattern goes on, so the operation involved is most likely addition or multiplication.

Answer: The correct answer is **31**.

The difference between consecutive numbers in the pattern is **6**.
Add **6** to each number to find the next number in the pattern.
1 + **6** = 7, 7 + **6** = 13, 13 + **6** = 19, and 19 + **6** = 25.
Therefore, the next number is **25 + 6 = 31**.

8. What is the **missing number** in the pattern below?

80, 40, 20, _____ , 5

Hint #1:

The numbers in the pattern are **decreasing**. Therefore, check to see if the pattern involves subtracting or dividing by a number.

Hint #2:

Each number in the pattern is **half** of the number that came before it.

Answer: The correct answer is **10**.

The numbers in the pattern are **decreasing**. Because each number is **half** of the number that came before it, the numbers are being divided by **2**. Divide 20 by 2 to find the number in the blank: **20 ÷ 2 = 10**.

To check the answer, divide 10 by 2 to get 5, which is the last number in the pattern.

9. A rectangular picture frame is **8 inches wide** and **10 inches long**. What is the **perimeter** of the frame?

_____

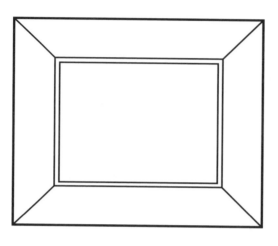

8 inches

10 inches

Hint #1:

Even though only two sides of the frame are mentioned in the question, the rectangular frame has **4 sides**.

Hint #2:

Use the formula: *Perimeter of a rectangle = (2 × length) + (2 × width)*.

Answer: The perimeter of the picture frame is **36 inches**.

Using the formula *Perimeter of a rectangle = (2 × length) + (2 × width)*, substitute **10** for the length and **8** for the width.

Perimeter of a rectangle = (2 × length) + (2 × width)
$$= (2 \times 10) + (2 \times 8)$$
$$= (20) + (16)$$
$$= 36 \text{ inches}$$

© Kaplan Publishing, Inc.

10. Which is the **next figure** in the pattern?

Ⓐ

Ⓑ

Ⓒ

Ⓓ None of these

Hint #1:

Find the **pattern** in the sequence. There are 3 figures that keep repeating to form the pattern.

Hint #2:

The **last triangle** in the sequence is shaded at the top. Find the answer choice that follows the one that is shaded at the top.

Answer: Choice **C** is correct.

There are 3 triangles in the pattern. The **first one** is shaded at the **top**, the **second one** is shaded at the **bottom** on the **right**, and the **third one** is shaded at the **bottom** on the **left**. The last triangle in the pattern is shaded at the **top**. So, the next triangle would be shaded at the bottom on the right, as is **choice C**.

11. What is the next number in the pattern?

2, 4, 8, 16, _____

Hint #1:

The numbers are **increasing**, so the next number should be **greater than 16**.

Hint #2:

Even though the numbers in the pattern are all **even**, the pattern is **not** increasing by just adding 2 each time. To discover the pattern, find out what you do to **2** to get **4**, and what you do to **4** to get **8**, and so on.

Answer: The next number in the pattern is **32**.

This is an example of a doubling pattern. Each time you are multiplying by 2 to get the next number in the pattern. Therefore, the number after 16 is **16 × 2 = 32**.

12. What is the value of the expression below when $x = 4$?

$$\frac{16 + x}{2 - 1}$$

_____

Hint #1:

Start by substituting **4** for **x**.
Then evaluate the expression.

Hint #2:

Evaluate the **numerator** first, then the **denominator**. The last step you will do is to **simplify** the fraction.

Answer: The correct answer is **20**.

First, substitute **x = 4** into the expression to get $\frac{16 + 4}{2 - 1}$.

Then, add **16 + 4** to get **20** in the numerator. Then, simplify the denominator to get **2 − 1 = 1**. The expression becomes $\frac{20}{1} = 20$.

13. Which figure is **missing** in the pattern below?

Ⓐ

Ⓑ

Ⓒ

Ⓓ

Hint #1:

There are **4 different squares** that repeat in the pattern.

Hint #2:

Find the square that would follow the square shaded in the **lower right half**.

Answer: Choice **B** is correct.

In this pattern, **half** of each square is shaded. The missing figure follows the square where the **lower right half** is shaded, so find another place in the pattern where this same square appears. The second to last square shown in the pattern **also** has the **lower right half** shaded. The square after it, which is the last square shown in the pattern, will be the **same** as the missing square. This figure has the **lower left half** shaded, as in choice **B**.

14. Write the equation that means the same as "**a number minus five is ten**." Use n as the variable. Write your answer on the line below.

_____

Hint #1:

Since you are asked to write an **equation**, be sure to include an **equal sign** in the answer.

Hint #2:

Use the **key words**, such as "*a number*," "*minus*," and "*is*" to translate the statement.

Answer: The correct answer is $n - 5 = 10$.

"**A number minus five**" is written as $n - 5$. The last part of the statement "**is ten**" is written as $= 10$.

Putting this together, the correct equation is $n - 5 = 10$.

15. In the equation $n - 6 = 20$, what is the value of n?
Write your answer on the line below.

_____

Hint #1:

Remember, to solve an equation get the variable alone. Use the **inverse** of subtraction to do this.

Hint #2:

The inverse, or opposite, of **subtracting 6** is **adding 6**. Add 6 to each side of the equation to get n alone.

Answer: The value of n is **26**.

Add 6 to each side of the equation to get the variable alone:

$$
\begin{array}{rr}
n - 6 = & 20 \\
+\,6 = & +\,6 \\
\hline
n = & 26
\end{array}
$$

16. A rectangular sports field is **40 yards wide** and **120 yards long**. How many yards is the **perimeter** of this field?

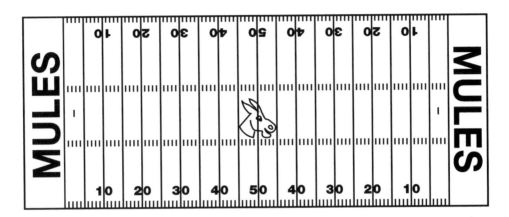

Hint #1:

Use the formula: *Perimeter of a rectangle = (2 × length) + (2 × width)*.

Hint #2:

Substitute **40** for the width and **120** for the length into the formula.

Answer: The perimeter is **320 yards**.

Using the formula *Perimeter of a rectangle = (2 × length) + (2 × width)*, substitute **120** for the length and **40** for the width.

Perimeter of a rectangle = (2 × *length*) + (2 × *width*)
= (2 × 120) + (2 × 40)
= (240) + (80)
= 320 yards

17. Evaluate the expression for $n = 8$:

$$n + 7 \times 4 \div 14$$

Write your answer on the line below.

_____

Hint #1:

First, substitute **8** for the letter **_n_**.

Hint #2:

Remember to evaluate using the order of operations (**PEMDAS**).

Answer: The correct answer is **10**.

First, substitute **_n_ = 8** to get **8 + 7 × 4 ÷ 14**.
Next, multiply to get **8 + 28 ÷ 14**.
In the next step, divide **28** by **14** to make the expression **8 + 2**.
Finally, add **8 + 2** for an answer of **10**.

18. In the equation $n \times 3 = 45$, what is the value of n?
Write your answer on the line below.

_____

Hint #1:

Remember, to solve an equation, get the variable alone. Use the **inverse** of multiplication to solve this question.

Hint #2:

The inverse, or opposite, of **multiplying by 3** is **dividing by 3**.

Answer: The correct answer is **15**.

Divide each side of the equation by 3 to get the variable alone.

$$
\begin{aligned}
n \times 3 &= \ \ 45 \\
\div 3 &= \div 3 \\
\hline
n &= \ \ 15
\end{aligned}
$$

19. Jacob has **16 piles** of pennies. Each pile has the same number of pennies. He has a total of **272 pennies**.

Write a **number sentence** that could be used to solve for the number of pennies in each of Jacob's piles, using n as a variable.

_____

Hint #1:

Multiply the number of pennies in each pile by the number of piles to get the total number of pennies. Since you are looking for the number of pennies in each pile, use a box, circle, or letter to represent this number in the number sentence.

Hint #2:

This number sentence can also be written using **division**.

Answer: Correct number sentences include: $16 \times n = 272$, or $272 \div 16 = n$.

In order to write the number sentence, multiply the total number of piles by the number of pennies in each pile.

The number of piles is **16**, and the number of pennies in each pile is not known. So this part of the sentence is **16 × n**. Set this expression equal to the total number of pennies, which is **272**. The statement becomes **16 × n = 272**.

The statement can also be written using division. Divide the total number of pennies (**272**) by the total number of piles (**16**) to get the number of pennies in each pile (**n**), or **272 ÷ 16 = n**.

© Kaplan Publishing, Inc.

You're doing a great job so far!
Are you ready for a Challenge Activity?

Good luck!

Look at the pattern below.

2, 7, 12, 17, _____ , _____ , _____

a) Describe the **rule** for the pattern in your own words.

_____

_____

_____

_____

b) Using the rule, what are the **next three numbers** in the pattern?

_____ , _____ , _____

c) If *n* represents any number in this pattern, **write a rule** that could be used to find the number after *n* in the pattern.

_____

_____

_____

_____

_____

See hints and answers on following page.

Answers to Challenge Activity:

a) The words in your rule may vary a bit, but the basic rule is:
   5 is being added to each number to get the next number in the pattern. For example, $2 + 5 = 7$, $7 + 5 = 12$, $12 + 5 = 17$, and so on.

b) Using your rule, the next three numbers in the pattern are **22**, **27**, and **32**. Start with the last number in the pattern, which is **17**. Add **5** to 17, and then add **5** to each new number in the pattern.
   $17 + 5 = 22$, $22 + 5 = 27$, and $27 + 5 = 32$.

c) The rule is ***n* + 5**.
   Each number in the pattern is the result of adding **5** to the number that came before it. The correct way to write this using ***n*** to represent the previous number in the pattern is ***n* + 5**.

Let's take a quick test and see how much you've learned during this climb up *SCORE!* Mountain.

Good luck!

1. In the equation $n \div 2 = 10$, what is the value of n?

_____

2. Kyle's rectangular yard has a length of 50 feet and a width of 30 feet. What is the perimeter of his yard?

_____

3. What is the next number in the pattern below?

2, 5, 8, 11, 14, _____

4. Which of the following means the same as the equation below?

$$n + 25 = 35$$

(A) The product of a number and 25 is equal to 35.

(B) The sum of a number and 25 is equal to 35.

(C) The quotient of a number and 25 is equal to 35.

(D) The difference of a number and 25 is equal to 35.

5. Evaluate the expression for $n = 16$.

$$(n - 4) + (20 \div 5) - 1$$

_____

Answers to test questions:

1. The correct answer is **20**.
   Multiply by 2 on each side of the equation to get the variable alone.

   $$n \div 2 = 10$$
   $$\underline{\times\, 2 = \times\, 2}$$
   $$n = \quad 20$$

2. The perimeter is **160 feet**.
   Using the formula ***Perimeter of a rectangle* = (2 × *length*) + (2 × *width*)**, substitute **50** for the length and **30** for the width.

   ***Perimeter of rectangle* = (2 × *length*) + (2 × *width*)**
   = (2 × 50) + (2 × 30)
   = (100) + (60)
   = 160 feet

3. The next number in the pattern is **17**.
   The numbers in the pattern are getting **larger by 3** each time. To find the next number, add **3** to the last number in the pattern: **14 + 3 = 17**.

4. Choice **B** is correct.
   ***n* + 25 = 35** means **the sum of a number and 25 is equal to 35**.
   The word ***sum*** is a key word for addition. In the equation above, ***n*** and 25 are being added to give a result of **35**.

5. The correct answer is **15**.
   To solve this problem, substitute for the variable and follow the order of operations. This order can be remembered with **PEMDAS**: **P**arentheses, **E**xponents, **M**ultiply and **D**ivide, **A**dd and **S**ubtract.
   First, substitute ***n* = 16** to get the expression **(16 − 4) + (20 ÷ 5) − 1**.
   Next, evaluate the parentheses. Since **16 − 4 = 12** and **20 ÷ 5 = 4**, the expression becomes **12 + 4 − 1**.
   Now, evaluate in order from left to right. **12 + 4 = 16** and **16 − 1 = 15**.

Celebrate!

Let's take a fun break before we go to the next base camp. You've earned it!

Take some time to visit your favorite park or school playground.

Congratulations!
You're getting closer to the top of *SCORE!* Mountain.

Get some fresh air and exercise!

Many times, parks have lots of great games, sports, and activities available.

Join in on the fun!

Get help from an adult to find out about different organized activities you can participate in.

Be sure to take a friend or relative when you go to share the good time!

Good luck and have fun!

You deserve it for working so hard!

Base Camp

5

Probability and Statistics

You are really getting close to the top of *SCORE!* Mountain. Great work! Let's keep going! Good luck!

SCORE! MOUNTAIN TOP

BASE CAMP 5

BASE CAMP 4

BASE CAMP 3

BASE CAMP 2

BASE CAMP 1

1. What is the **mean** of the following set of numbers?

10, 34, 16, 19, 31, 40

Write your answer on the line below.

_____

Hint #1:

The **mean** is the average of a set of numbers.

Hint #2:

The **first step** in finding the mean is to find the **sum** of the set of numbers. The **second step** is to **divide** the sum by the total number of items in the set.

Answer: The mean of the set of numbers is **25**.

A quick way to find the sum of the numbers in the set is to add compatible numbers first. In this question, 10 + 40 = **50**, 34 +16 = **50**, and 19 + 31 = **50**. **50 + 50 + 50 = 150**.

Divide this total by the number of addends, which is **6. 150 ÷ 6 = 25**

2. There are a total of **24 students** in Ciara's class. Of these 24 students, **13** are **boys**. If one student is selected at random to represent the class, what is the **probability** that this student is a **girl**?

_____

Hint #1:

To find the **probability** of an event, first figure out the total number of ways the event can happen. In this case, the event is choosing a girl at random from Ciara's class. First, find the **total number** of girls. Then, **divide** this number by the **total number** of possibilities. Here, the total number of possibilities is the total number of students in the class.

Hint #2:

Since the number of boys was given, **subtract** this number from the total students in the class to find the number of girls. Place this number over the total number of students in the class to write the probability.

Answer: The probability of selecting a girl at random from Ciara's class is $\frac{11}{24}$.

The probability of an event happening is equal to

$$\frac{\text{the number of ways the event can happen}}{\text{the total number of possibilities}}.$$

Because there are **13 boys** out of **24 students**, there are **24 − 13 = 11 girls** in the class. The probability of a girl being selected is equal to

$$\frac{\text{the number of girls in the class}}{\text{the total number of students}} = \frac{11}{24}.$$

3. The heights in inches of 5 students were measured and recorded:

63 inches   58 inches   59 inches   65 inches   70 inches

What is the **mean** height of these students?
Write your answer on the line below.

_____

Hint #1:

To find the **mean**, first find the **sum** of the numbers.

Hint #2:

The second step is to **divide** the sum by the total number of addends.

Answer: The mean height of these students is **63 inches**.

Add the values **63 + 58 + 59 + 65 + 70**.
Then, divide this sum by **5** to find the average height.
63 + 58 + 59 + 65 + 70 = 315, 315 ÷ 5 = 63 inches

4. The **graph** below shows the number of students buying lunch each day of one week.

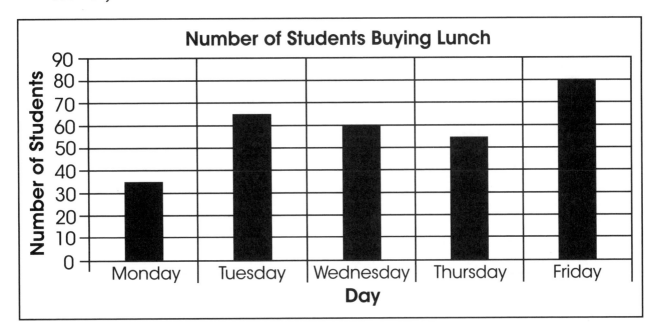

Number of Students Buying Lunch

What is the **total** number of students buying lunch on **Wednesday** and **Friday**? Write your answer on the line below.

_____

Hint #1:

To find the total number, find the **sum** of the lunches bought on those days.

Hint #2:

Locate the point on the graph above **Wednesday** and **add** this number to the number for the point on the graph above **Friday**.

Answer: The total number of lunches sold on Wednesday and Friday is **140**.

80 students bought lunch on Friday, and **60** students bought lunch on Wednesday. To find the total for these two days, add: **60 + 80 = 140 lunches**.

5. The **table** below shows the results of a student survey. Each student was asked about his or her favorite lunch.

Students' Favorite Lunches

Type of Lunch	Number of Students
pizza	15
hot dog	13
hamburger	10
peanut butter and jelly	12

If each student surveyed chose only **one lunch**, how many students answered the survey?
Write your answer on the line below.

_____

Hint #1:

First, find the total number of students for each choice in the table.

Hint #2:

Next, find the **sum** of the numbers in the table.

Answer: A total of **50 students** answered the survey.

The total for **pizza** is **15**, **hot dog** is **13**, **hamburger** is **10**, and **peanut butter and jelly** is **12**. Add the totals for each lunch: **15 + 13 + 10 + 12 = 50 students**.

6. Using the data table from question 5, construct a **bar graph** of the information. Include all labels.

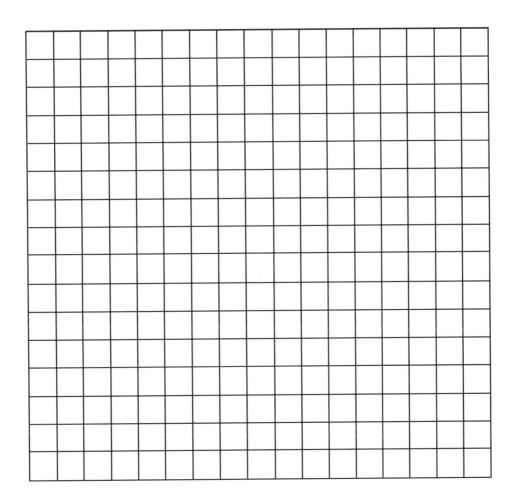

© Kaplan Publishing, Inc.

Hint #1:

Start by choosing a **scale** for the **vertical axis**. Make each bar worth **one unit**. Be sure to make the height of each bar match the numbers from the table.

Hint #2:

Be sure to **label** each **axis**, and give the graph a **title**.

See answers on following page.

Answer: **Your graph should be similar to the graph shown below:**

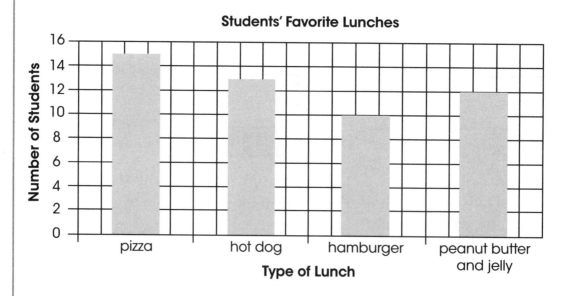

Be sure that your graph has a **bar** for **each** lunch choice, has an appropriate, **vertical scale**, each **axis** is **labeled**, and there is a **title** for the graph.

7. While playing a board game, Tina is rolling a **standard six-sided** number cube. On the line below, make a **list of possible outcomes** when Tina rolls the cube.

_____

Hint #1:

If there are 6 sides on the cube, then the **list of outcomes** should include **6 possibilities**.

Hint #2:

The smallest number on a standard number cube is **1** and the greatest number is **6**.

Answer: The correct answer is {**1, 2, 3, 4, 5, 6**}.

The **list of possible outcomes** is the set of all possibilities after the cube is rolled. Since there are **6 sides** to a number cube, there are **6 different outcomes**.

8. When rolling a number cube, what is the **probability** of getting an **even number** on the cube? Write your answer on the line below.

_____

Hint #1:

The probability of an event happening is equal to:

$$P(event) = \frac{\text{the number of ways the event can happen}}{\text{the total number of possibilities}}.$$

Hint #2:

Remember, there are **6 sides** to a number cube so **6** is the total number of possibilities.

Answer: The **probability** of getting an **even number** on the cube is $\frac{3}{6}$ or $\frac{1}{2}$.

The **even numbers** on a number cube are **2**, **4**, and **6**; so there are **3 ways** to get an even number. The **probability** of getting an even number is equal to P(even number) $= \frac{\text{the number of ways the event can happen}}{\text{the total number of possibilities}}$, which is also equal to $\frac{1}{2}$.

© Kaplan Publishing, Inc.

9. When rolling a number cube, what is the **probability** of getting a **prime number**?
Write your answer on the line below.

_____

Hint #1:

Remember, the formula for figuring out the probability of an event happening is equal to:

$$P(\text{event}) = \frac{\text{the number of ways the event can happen}}{\text{the total number of possibilities}}.$$

Hint #2:

A **prime number** has **exactly** two different factors that are **integers**. The number **1** is **neither** prime nor composite.

Answer: The correct answer is $\frac{3}{6}$ or $\frac{1}{2}$.

Find the **total** number of prime numbers on the cube and use this as the **numerator** of the fraction. There are **3** prime numbers on a number cube: **2**, **3**, and **5**, and there are a total of **6** sides on the cube.

Therefore, the probability is $\frac{3}{6}$, which can be simplified to $\frac{1}{2}$.

10. The number of students at an after school club is shown below.

25 on Monday
30 on Tuesday
24 on Wednesday
29 on Thursday
17 on Friday

What is the **mean** number of students at the club for these five days? Write your answer on the line below.

_____

Hint #1:

Remember, to find the mean, find the **sum** of the list of numbers and then **divide** the sum by the total number of values in the list.

Hint #2:

Find the sum by adding the daily student totals for each of the five days.

Answer: The **mean** number of students at the club for these five days is **25**.

First, find the sum of the list of numbers.
The sum of **25 + 30 + 24 + 29 + 17** is **125**.
Then divide by the total number of days: **125 ÷ 5 = 25 students**.

11. On his way home from school, Tim started off running. When he had gone **halfway** home, he got tired and walked the rest of the way. Which of the **graphs** below **best** represents Tim's trip home?

Ⓐ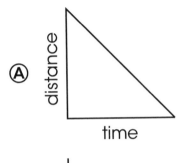

Ⓑ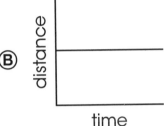

Ⓒ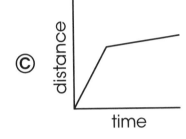

Ⓓ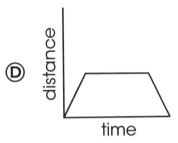

Hint #1:

The **faster** Tim traveled, the **steeper** the line should be.

Hint #2:

Tim did **not** go the same speed the entire time. Look for the graph the shows a **faster** speed at the **start** of his trip, and a **slower** speed for the **second half** of the trip.

Answer: The correct answer is choice **C**.

This graph shows a **steeper** line for the **first part** of the graph. This is the section of the graph where he was running. The line then gets **less steep** for the **second half** of the graph. This shows the part of his trip that he was walking.

12. The following table shows the number of students at Franklin School in Grades 4 and 5 who participate in **band** and **chorus**.

Grade Level	4th	5th
band	35	37
chorus	48	51

If each student can be a member of **only one group**, what is the **total** number of students involved in band and chorus in **both grades**? Write your answer on the line below.

_____

Hint #1:

Take the **total** students involved in each group for each grade and find the **sum**.

Hint #2:

Don't forget that each student can be a member of only **one group**!

© Kaplan Publishing, Inc.

Answer: The total number of students involved in band and chorus in both grades is **171**.

To find the total number of students involved in both groups, add the numbers in the table for each group and each grade level.
35 + 37 + 48 + 51 = 171 students.

13. The **table** below shows the number of people who went to the movies during one week.

Day of the week	Number of people
Thursday	80
Friday	100
Saturday	140
Sunday	120

Construct a **bar graph** of the information in the table.

Answer: The height of your graph may differ, depending on the scale you used.

One correct answer for the bar graph is shown below:

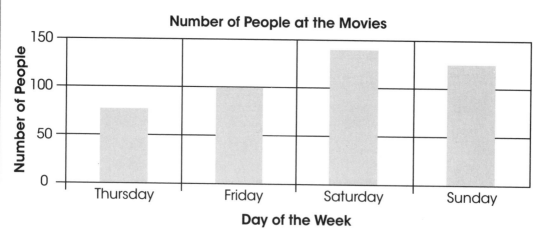

Be sure that your graph has a **bar** for each day, has an appropriate **vertical scale**, and has each **axis** labeled. Finally, make sure to give your graph a **title**!

14. Stacie is ordering **ice cream** at a restaurant.

She has a choice between a **cone** and a **dish**.
She can choose **vanilla, chocolate,** or **strawberry** ice cream.

If she selects **one flavor** of ice cream, how many **different** ice cream desserts are possible?
Write your answer on the line below.

_____

Hint #1:

Stacie can choose from **3** different flavors. Each flavor can be served **2** different ways: in a cone or a dish. **Multiply** the number of flavors by the number of ways the ice cream can be served to solve the problem.

Hint #2:

Another way to solve this is to make an **organized list** of the different possibilities. Then count the number of possibilities in the list to get the answer.

Answer: Stacie can order **6 different ice cream desserts**.

Using the **counting principle**, multiply **2** serving choices by **3** flavors to get $2 \times 3 = 6$ **different desserts**.

Another strategy is to make an **organized list** of the possibilities. Pair up each ice cream flavor with cone and dish:

    1. vanilla in a cone
    2. vanilla in a dish
    3. chocolate in a cone
    4. chocolate in a dish
    5. strawberry in a cone
    6. strawberry in a dish

There are a total of **6 different desserts** in this list.

15. Using the information in question 14, what is the **probability** of Stacie randomly selecting **chocolate ice cream in a dish**?

Write your answer on the line below.

_____

Hint #1:

Remember, the probability of an event happening is equal to:

$$P(\text{event}) = \frac{\text{the number of ways the event can happen}}{\text{the total number of possibilities}}.$$

Hint #2:

You discovered in question 14 that there are a **total** of **6** different dessert possibilities and only **1** dessert listed as **chocolate ice cream in a dish**.

Answer: The probability of Stacie randomly selecting chocolate ice cream in a dish is $\frac{1}{6}$.

There is only **1** dessert listed as chocolate ice cream in a dish out of a total of **6** possibilities. Enter this information into the probability formula:

$$P(\text{event}) = \frac{\text{the number of ways the event can happen}}{\text{the total number of possibilities}} \text{ and you get } \frac{1}{6}.$$

16. The **graph** below shows the number of books read by Mrs. Wood's class over a period of **5 weeks**.

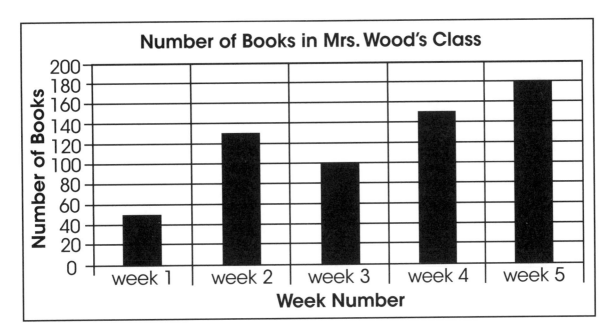

Number of Books in Mrs. Wood's Class

How many **more** books were read during **week** 4 than **week** 3?

Write your answer on the line below.

_____

Hint #1:

First compare the data in the graph for **week 3** and **week 4**.

Hint #2:

Use **subtraction** to find the difference in the number of books read for these two weeks.

Answer: 50 more books were read during week 4 than week 3.

The dot on the graph for the number of books read during week 4 is halfway between **140** and **160**. Therefore, the number of books read during week 4 is **150**. The number of books read during week 3 is **100**.
150 − 100 = 50 books

17. Using the graph in question 16, what is the **total number** of books read in Mrs. Wood's class during the **entire** 5-week period?
Write your answer on the line below.

_____

Hint #1:

First, find the number of books read during each of the 5 weeks.

Hint #2:

To solve the problem, **add** the number of books read each week to get the total for the entire 5-week period.

Answer: A total of **610 books** were read during the entire 5-week period.

The total for **week 1** on the graph is halfway between 40 and 60, so week 1 is equal to **50 books**.

The total for **week 2** is halfway between 120 and 140, so week 2 is equal to **130 books**.

You learned from question 16 that the total for **week 3** is **100 books** and the total for **week 4** is **150 books**.

The total for **week 5** is **180 books**.

Find the sum of numbers for the 5 weeks:
50 + 130 + 100 + 150 + 180 = 610 books

18. At a store, there are shirts in **3** different sizes: **small, medium,** and **large**. The shirts come in **red, blue,** or **green**.

How many different shirts are available at this store? Write your answer on the line below.

_____

Hint #1:

There are **3** different sizes of shirts in **3** different colors. You can use the **counting principle** and multiply the total number of choices to find the total number of available

Hint #2:

You can also make an **organized list** of all of the possibilities. Count the number of shirts in the list to find the answer.

Answer: The correct answer is **9 shirts**.

Using the counting principle, multiply **3** sizes by **3** colors to get **3 × 3 = 9** different shirts.

Another strategy to use in the problem is to make an organized list of the possibilities:

1. small red shirt
2. medium red shirt
3. large red shirt
4. small blue shirt
5. medium blue shirt
6. large blue shirt
7. small green shirt
8. medium green shirt
9. large green shirt

By counting the number of items on the list, you can see that there are **9 different shirts** available at the store.

19. Using the information from question 18, what is the **probability** of selecting an **orange** shirt in size **medium**?

_____

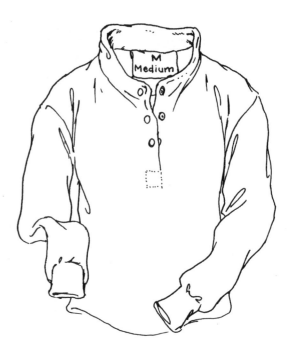

Hint #1:

The probability of an event happening is equal to:

$$P(\text{event}) = \frac{\text{the number of ways the event can happen}}{\text{the total number of possibilities}}.$$

Hint #2:

Count the number of possible medium orange shirt combinations. This number will be the **numerator** of the fraction. The total number of shirt choices available at the store will be the **denominator** of the fraction.

Answer: The correct answer is $\frac{0}{9}$ or **0**.

There are **zero** orange shirts at this store. Therefore, it is **impossible** to select an orange shirt in any size. The probability of any impossible event is **always** zero.

Challenge Activity

You're doing a great job so far!
Are you ready for a Challenge Activity?

Good luck!

1 green six-sided number cube and 1 red six-sided number cube are rolled at the same time.

a) What is the **probability** of rolling a **sum of** 4?

_____

b) What is the probability of rolling the **same number** on each cube?

_____

c) What is the probability of getting a **sum of 4** or **the same number** on each cube?

_____

Hint #1:

Make an **organized list** of the possibilities when rolling two number cubes at the same time. When two number cubes are rolled, there are a total of **36 possible outcomes**.

Hint #2:

The outcome of getting a **2** on both cubes is counted in **both situations** and cannot be counted **twice in part c**.

See answers on following page.

© Kaplan Publishing, Inc.

Answers to Challenge Activity:

To begin, make an organized list of all the possible outcomes when rolling the cubes. The table below is a list of the 36 possibilities.

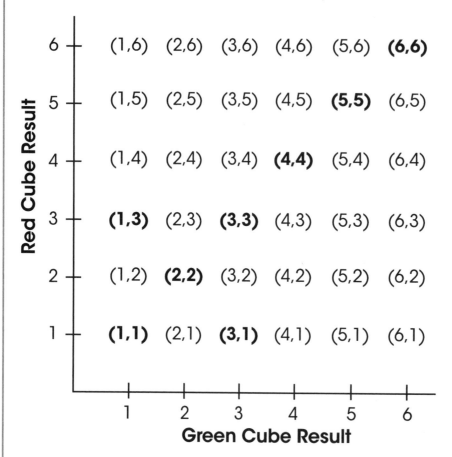

Red Cube Result

6   (1,6)   (2,6)   (3,6)   (4,6)   (5,6)   **(6,6)**

5   (1,5)   (2,5)   (3,5)   (4,5)   **(5,5)**   (6,5)

4   (1,4)   (2,4)   (3,4)   **(4,4)**   (5,4)   (6,4)

3   **(1,3)**   (2,3)   **(3,3)**   (4,3)   (5,3)   (6,3)

2   (1,2)   **(2,2)**   (3,2)   (4,2)   (5,2)   (6,2)

1   **(1,1)**   (2,1)   **(3,1)**   (4,1)   (5,1)   (6,1)

          1   2   3   4   5   6

Green Cube Result

a) The probability of rolling a sum of 4 is $\frac{3}{36} = \frac{1}{12}$.

In the list of outcomes in the table above, there are **3** ways to get a **sum of 4**:
Rolling a **1** on the green cube and a **3** on the red cube.
Rolling a **1** on the red cube and **3** on the green cube.
Rolling a **2** on each cube.

Recall that the probability of an event happening is equal to:

$$P(\text{event}) = \frac{\text{the number of ways the event can happen}}{\text{the total number of possibilities}}.$$

Because there are **3** ways to get a **sum of 4**, and the total number of possibilities shown in the table is 36, the probability is equal to $\frac{3}{36}$, which simplifies to $\frac{1}{12}$.

Answers to Challenge Activity, *continued*:

b) The probability of rolling the **same number** on each cube is $\frac{6}{36} = \frac{1}{6}$. There are **6 ways** to get the same number on each cube:

1 and **1**, **2** and **2**, **3** and **3**, **4** and **4**, **5** and **5**, and **6** and **6**.

The **probability** is $\frac{6}{36}$, which simplifies to $\frac{1}{6}$.

c) The probability of getting a **sum of 4** or **the same number** on each cube is $\frac{8}{36} = \frac{2}{9}$.

Be careful on this part of the question. There are **3 ways** to make a **sum of 4**. There are **6 ways** to get the **same number** on each cube. But as **Hint #2** says, the outcome of getting a **2** on both cubes is counted in **each of these situations**. Because it **cannot** be counted **twice** when calculating the joint probability, count the **3 ways** to get a **sum of four** and **5 other ways** to get **the same number** on each cube.

The probability is $\frac{3}{36} + \frac{5}{36} = \frac{8}{36}$, which simplifies to $\frac{2}{9}$.

Let's take a quick test and see how much you've learned during this climb up *SCORE!* Mountain.

Good luck!

1. Below are the number of sit-ups done in 1 minute for 6 students.

25   36   23   33   40   29

What is the mean number of sit-ups for these 6 students?

_____

2. The chart below shows three different activities for Play Session 1 at a camp and the number of boys and girls who participated in them.

Activity	Boys	Girls
swim	20	15
bike	15	13
crafts	10	10

If a child can only participate in one activity during Play Session 1, what is the total number of students who participated in swim or bike activities for Play Session 1?

_____

© Kaplan Publishing, Inc.

3. The bar graph below shows the total number of yearbooks sold at Torwood Middle School over 3 days.

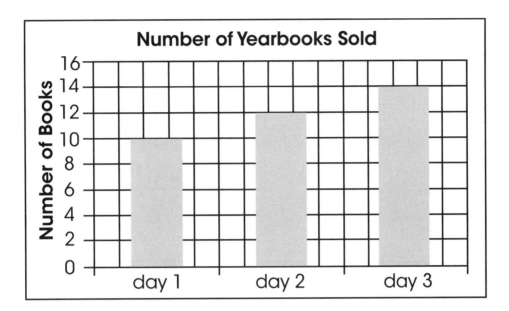

Number of Yearbooks Sold

If this trend continues, what should be the total number of yearbooks sold on the 5th day?

_____

4. While playing a game, Kylie used a spinner like the one below.

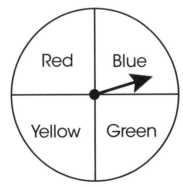

What is the outcome set, or list of possible outcomes, for spinning this spinner?

_____

5. Using the spinner from question 4, what is the probability of getting red or blue when spinning the spinner once?

_____

Answers to test questions:

1. The correct answer is **31**.

First, find the total number of sit-ups done by the six students:
25 + 36 + 23 + 33 + 40 + 29 = 186.
Then, divide by the total number of students: **186 ÷ 6 = 31 sit-ups.**

2. The correct answer is **90 students**.

Add the total number of boys and girls for the **swim** and **bike** activities from the table. **20 + 30 + 15 + 25 = 90 students.**

3. The correct answer is **18 yearbooks**.

There were **10** yearbooks sold on **day 1**, **12** sold on **day 2**, and **14** sold on **day 3**. Each day there are **2 more** yearbooks sold than on the **previous day**. Therefore, if this trend continues there will be **14 + 2 = 16 yearbooks** sold on **day 4** and **16 + 2 = 18 yearbooks** sold on **day 5**.

4. The correct answer is **{red, blue, green, yellow}**.

The **outcome set** is the list of possible outcomes for an event. To find the outcome set, make a list of all the possible results when spinning the spinner and write it as a set. In this case the set includes the four colors on the spinner.

Answers to test questions, *continued*:

5. The probability of getting red or blue when spinning the spinner once is $\frac{2}{4}$ or $\frac{1}{2}$.

There are **4 possible outcomes** on the spinner. Because the sections for each color are the **same size**, the chance of getting each color is the **same**.

The probability of an event is equal to:

$$P(\text{event}) = \frac{\text{the number of ways the event can happen}}{\text{the total number of possibilities}}.$$

There is **1 red section** and **1 blue section**, so there are 2 ways for the event to happen. This is the **numerator** of your fraction.
There are a total of **4 sections** to the spinner, so there are **4 different possibilities**. This is the **denominator** of your fraction.

This makes the probability equal to $\frac{2}{4}$, which simplifies to $\frac{1}{2}$.

Celebrate!

Let's take a fun break before we go to the next base camp. You've earned it!

Congratulations!
You're almost to the top of *SCORE!* Mountain.

Let's make a **scrapbook**!

What you need:

- Some of your favorite photos. First ask your parents for permission to include these photos in your scrapbook!

- Glue

- Paper or an empty photo album

- Things to decorate your pages, like stickers, magic markers, or anything else you want to use!

Scrapbooking is an excellent way to preserve fond memories!

It's also a fun break from studying!

You can use a blank photo album or even just plain paper.

Paste your favorite pictures onto each page, and use markers, stickers, or anything else you have to decorate.

Next to each photo, write down your thoughts and memories about each picture. It's a great way to remember special times in your life!

When you're finished, share your scrapbook with your family and friends!

Good luck and have fun!
You deserve it for working so hard!

Base Camp

6

Everyday Math

You've made it to the final base camp! Outstanding! Make it through and you'll be at the top of *SCORE!* Mountain. You can do it. Good luck!

SCORE! MOUNTAIN TOP

BASE CAMP 5

BASE CAMP 4

BASE CAMP 3

BASE CAMP 2

BASE CAMP 1

1. Ethan mowed lawns last summer and earned **$20 per lawn**. Each tank of gas cost **$15**. If he mowed **10 lawns each week** and used **3 tanks of gas per week**, what was the **total** amount of money he earned each week after paying for gas? Write your answer on the line below.

_____

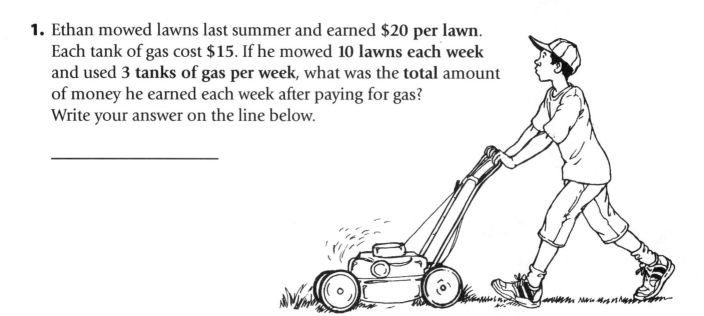

Hint #1:

One way to solve this problem is to break it up into three steps. The **first step** will be to calculate how much money Ethan earned mowing the 10 lawns. The **second step** will be to find the amount of money he spent on gas. The **third step** will be to subtract the money he spent on gas from the money he earned mowing the 10 lawns.

Hint #2:

You can write an **expression**. For this problem, Ethan made **$20** mowing **10** lawns but spent **$15** each for **3** tanks of gas. Therefore, you can set up the expression **20 × 10 − 15 × 3** to solve it. Be sure to use the order of operations when figuring out the answer!

Answer: Ethan earned a total of **$155** each week after paying for gas.

He made **$20 × 10 = $200** but had to spend **$15 × 3 = $45** on gas. Therefore, the money he earned is **$200 − $45 = $155**.

2. At Riverdale Academy, the lockers are numbered in order from **1 to 100**. If each of the lockers is open, and a student walking down the hallway closes each locker that is a **multiple of** 3, how many lockers does she close? Write your answer on the line below.

_____

Hint #1:

Try looking for a **pattern**. Count the **multiples of 3** from **1 to 30** first. They are **3, 6, 9, 12, 15, 18, 21, 24, 27**, and **30**. Use this pattern to help you figure out the multiples of **3** from **31 to 60**, and then from **61 to 100**.

Hint #2:

You can also **divide the total number of lockers by 3** to get the correct answer. You must round your answer down however, because you cannot have a fraction of a locker!

Answer: The correct answer is **33 lockers**.

There are **33 multiples of 3** from 1 to 100, so the student must close **33 lockers**!

3. On Elm Street, the houses are numbered from 240 to 270. Charles delivers newspapers to each house whose number is a **multiple of 6**. How many houses does he deliver to on this street? Write your answer on the line below.

_____

Hint #1:

One way to solve this problem is to make an **organized list**. Start with the smallest **multiple of 6** in this list and make a list of all the houses on Elm Street whose numbers are a multiple of 6.

Hint #2:

Multiples of 6 are even numbers that are also multiples of 3. The smallest multiple of 6 in this list is 240.

Answer: Charles delivers newspapers to **6 houses** on Elm Street.

When making an organized list of the **multiples of 6**, start with **240**, since **6 × 40 = 240**. When completed, your list should have the following 6 house numbers: **240, 246, 252, 258, 264,** and **270.**

4. Sara is making cookies and is using a recipe that makes **24 cookies**. The recipe calls for 1 cup of sugar. If she wants to make **60 cookies**, how much **sugar** should she use? Write your answer on the line below.

_____

Hint #1:

Try making a **table** to solve this problem.

Hint #2:

When putting together your table, have one column list the **number of cookies** the recipe makes. In the other column, list the **amount of sugar** necessary.

Answer: Sara should use $2\frac{1}{2}$ **cups** of sugar to make 60 cookies.

Did you try making a **table** to solve this problem?

Number of cookies	24	36	48	60
Cups of sugar needed	1	$1\frac{1}{2}$	2	$2\frac{1}{2}$

To make **60 cookies**, Sara will multiply the recipe amounts by $2\frac{1}{2}$, since 60 is $2\frac{1}{2}$ times 24. **1 cup $\times$ $2\frac{1}{2}$ is $2\frac{1}{2}$ cups of sugar.**

5. Sarah wants to buy **3 shirts** that cost **$14.95 each**. If she has **$50.00** to spend, does she have enough money to buy all 3 shirts? Write your answer on the line below.

_____

Hint #1:

One way to solve this problem is to use rounded, simpler numbers.

Hint #2:

Round $14.95 to **$15.00**. Then use that amount to determine if Sarah has enough money.

Answer: Yes, Sarah has enough money to buy all 3 shirts.

By using the hints and rounding the cost of each shirt, it would cost **$15.00 × 3 = $45.00** to buy all 3 shirts. Since Sarah has **$50.00** to spend, she will have enough money.

6. There will be **128 people** at the school picnic. Each person at the picnic will get **2 sandwiches**. There are **212 sandwiches** already made. How many sandwiches still need to be made for the picnic? Write your answer on the line below.

_____

Hint #1:

This is a multistep problem. The key to solving it is to choose the proper **mathematical operation** to figure out each step.

Hint #2:

Because each person will get **2 sandwiches**, first choose an operation to figure out the **total** number of sandwiches needed at the picnic. Then, find the **difference** between the number of sandwiches needed and the number already made.

Answer: 44 sandwiches still need to be made for the picnic.

The operations needed for this problem are **multiplication** and **subtraction**. To find the **total** number of sandwiches needed, multiply **2 × 128 people**. This gives a total of 256 sandwiches.

To figure out how many sandwiches still need to be made, subtract: **256 − 212 = 44 sandwiches**.

7. At Springville School, 54 **students** play **soccer** and 35 **students** play **football**. If 26 **students** play both soccer and football, how many students play soccer only? Write your answer on the line below.

_____

Hint #1:

A good way to solve this problem would be to draw a **Venn diagram**.

Hint #2:

When constructing a Venn diagram, remember to use **2 interlocking circles**. Label one circle **Soccer** and the other one **Football**. The place where the circles overlap should be labeled with the number of students who play **both sports**.

Answer: 28 students play soccer only.

If you used a Venn diagram to solve this problem, it should look something like this:

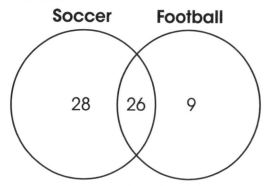

The circle for **soccer** is made up of **two sections**: the soccer only part and the part that overlaps with the circle for football.

The number of students who play both sports and the number of soccer only students should add to a total of **54**.

Subtract the number of students who play both sports from the total number who play soccer.

54 − 26 = 28 students who play soccer only.

8. Stanley, Barbara, and Jesse each have a different **favorite subject**.

One likes **math** the best, one likes **science** the best, and one enjoys **history** the most.

Stanley does **not** like math or history.
Jesse likes to work with numbers.
What is **Barbara's** favorite subject?
Write your answer on the line below.

_____

Hint #1:

Use **logical reasoning** to solve this problem. You are given information about what Stanley and Jesse like. By figuring out each of their favorite subjects, you can figure out what is Barbara's favorite subject by the process of elimination.

Hint #2:

It could help to make a **table** to solve this problem. Place **3 rows** and **3 columns** in your table. Have 1 row for **each person** and 1 column for **each subject**. Using the clues in the question put an **X** in each box that can be eliminated as a possibility.

Answer: Barbara's favorite subject is **history**.

If you made a table to solve this problem, it should look something like this:

	Math	Science	History
Stanley	X	✔	X
Barbara	X	X	✔
Jesse	✔	X	X

Use each clue to **cross out** possibilities in the table.
Stanley does not like math or history, so cross them out in his row.
Therefore, his favorite subject **must** be **science**. If his favorite subject is science, then cross it out for the other two people.
Jesse likes to work with numbers, so his favorite subject **must** be math.
That leaves **history** as Barbara's favorite subject.

9. Judy is reading a book for a report.

On the **first day**, she reads **3 pages**.
On the **second day,** she reads **6 pages**.
On the **third day**, she reads **9 pages**.

If this pattern continues, how many pages will she read on the **fifth day**?
Write your answer on the line below.

_____

Hint #1:

Try finding a **pattern** in how many pages Judy is reading each day.

Hint #2:

Once you figure out the pattern, continue it to the **5ᵗʰ day**.

Answer: If the pattern continues, Judy will read **15 pages** on the **5ᵗʰ** day.

She reads **3 more pages** each day than she read the day before. Continuing the pattern, she will read **12 pages** on the **4ᵗʰ day** and then **15 pages** on the **5ᵗʰ day**.

10. Ms. Brown is moving to a new classroom. She needs to pack **93 books** into boxes. Each box holds **12 books**.

How many boxes does Ms. Brown need to pack all the books? Write your answer on the line below.

_____

Hint #1:

The key to solving this problem is to figure out the correct math operation to use.

Hint #2:

Use **division** to solve this question. Be sure to consider the remainder when finding the total number of boxes.

Answer: Ms. Brown needs **8 boxes** to pack all of her books.

Divide **93 ÷ 12** to get **7 with a remainder of 9**.

Ms. Brown will need **7 full boxes** plus **one more** for the extra 9 books, for a total of **8 boxes**.

11. At a pet store, there are **twice** as many **cats** as **dogs**.

There are **three times** as many **birds** as **cats**.
There are **four times** as many **fish** as **birds**.
If there are **120 fish**, how many of **each animal** are there?

Fish _____

Birds _____

Cats _____

Dogs _____

Hint #1:

It might help to work **backward** in order to solve this problem.

Hint #2:

Start with the fact that there are **120 fish**. If there are four times as many fish than there are birds, then **120 ÷ 4** equals the number of birds. Continue this strategy to find the number of each animal at the pet store.

Answers:

Fish: **120**
Birds: **30**
Cats: **10**
Dogs: **5**

Start with the fact that there are **120 fish**. The question states that there are **four times** as many **fish** as **birds**. Working backward, divide the number of fish by **4** to find the number of birds. **120 ÷ 4 = 30 birds**

There are **three times** as many **birds** as **cats**. Working backward again, divide the number of birds by **3** to find the number of cats. **30 ÷ 3 = 10 cats**.

Because there are **twice** as many **cats** as **dogs**, divide the number of cats by **2** to find the number of dogs. **10 ÷ 2 = 5 dogs**

12. In a basketball tournament, **each team** plays every other team **once**. If there are **four teams** in the tournament (team **A, B, C,** and **D**), how many games **total** will be played? Write your answer on the line below.

_____

Hint #1:

Try **drawing a diagram** or looking for a **pattern** to help solve this problem.

Hint #2:

Remember, a game where **team A** plays **team B** is the **same** as a game where **team B** plays **team A**.

Answer: There will be a total of **6 games** played in the basketball tournament.

Team A will play **team B, C,** and **D** (**3 games**).
Team B will also play **teams C** and **D** (**2 games**).
Team C will still need to play **team D** (**1 game**).
All the possible games for **team D** are listed above.
This is a total of **3 + 2 + 1 = 6 games**.

Another way to look at this problem is to make a list of all the games that will be played:
   1. team A plays team B
   2. team A plays team C
   3. team A plays team D
   4. team B plays team C
   5. team B plays team D
   6. team C plays team D
   This gives you a total of **6 games**.

13. Chelsea used **39-cent** and **20-cent** stamps to mail a package. If the **total cost** of mailing the package was **$2.56** and she used a total of **9 stamps**, how many of each type of stamp did she use? Write your answer on the line below.

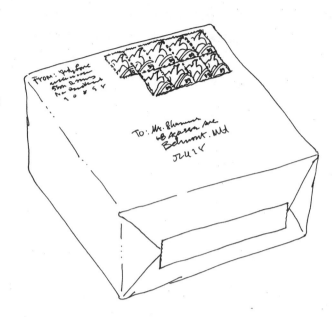

_____

Hint #1:

Try constructing a table and trying out different combinations of each type of stamp to figure out the correct answer.

Hint #2:

Be sure that the total number of stamps used is **9**.

Answer: Chelsea used **four 39-cent stamps** and **five 20-cent stamps**.

Try out different combinations of each type of stamp to get the answer, using a table to keep track of your guesses.

For example, you may start by guessing that there are **three 39-cent stamps** and **six 20-cent stamps**. Find the total value of these stamps: **3 × 0.39 = $1.17** and **6 × 0.20 = $1.20**. **$1.17 + $1.20 = $2.37**, which is **too low**.

Try your next guess with a **larger number** of the more expensive stamp. For the second guess, try **five 39-cent stamps** and **four 20-cent stamps**. Find the total value of these stamps: **5 × 0.39 = $1.95** and **4 × 0.20 = $0.80**. **$1.95 + 0.80 = $2.75**, which is closer, but **too high**.

Try the next guess with **fewer** of the more expensive stamp: **four 39-cent stamps** and **five 20-cent stamps**. Find the total value of these stamps: **4 × 0.39 = $1.56** and **5 × 0.20 = $1.00**. **$1.56 + $1.00 = $2.56**, which is the correct answer.

14. Ted is shopping at the market and needs paper towels. He can buy the 4-roll pack for **$3.00** or the 12-roll pack for **$8.40**.

Which pack should Ted buy if he wants to pay the **least amount** per roll? Write your answer on the line below.

_____

Hint #1:

Try finding the **unit prices** by finding the cost of one roll for **each pack** and then **comparing** the two prices to see which one is cheaper.

Hint #2:

To find the cost of one roll, **divide** the total cost of the pack by the number of rolls in the pack.

Answer: The **12-roll pack** is the best buy.

For the 4-roll pack: $3.00 ÷ 4 = **$0.75 per roll**.
For the 12-roll pack: $8.40 ÷ 12 = **$0.70 per roll**.
Therefore, it costs **less per roll** to buy the **12-roll pack** of paper towels.

15. At a restaurant, the different prices of items on the menu, including tax, are listed below.

Menu Item	Price
hamburger	$2.95
french fries	$1.85
salad	$2.69
soft drink	$0.99

Darnell wants to order a hamburger, french fries, and a drink for lunch. If he has **$5.00** to spend, does he have enough money to pay for his lunch? Write your answer on the line below.

_____

Hint #1:

Try simplifying the problem by **rounding** the costs of the items on the menu.

Hint #2:

Round the cost of each item and find the **total** cost of the three items combined. **Compare** this total amount with $5.00 to see if Darnell has enough money.

Answer: Darnell does **not** have enough money to pay for his lunch.

First, **round** the costs of each food item: a hamburger is around **$3.00**, French fries are about **$2.00**, a drink is around **$1.00**. Next, add these three amounts: **$3.00 + $2.00 + $1.00 = $6.00**.

Because Darnell only has **$5.00**, he does **not** have enough money to pay for these three items.

16. The line at an ice cream stand has **9 people** in it.

If it takes $1\frac{1}{2}$ minutes for each person to be served, how long will the wait be for the 9th person in line to get his or her ice cream? Write your answer on the line below.

_____

Hint #1:

The key to solving this problem is choosing the correct math operation to find the total wait time for the 9 people in the line.

Hint #2:

Use **multiplication** to solve this problem.

Answer: The correct answer is **$13\frac{1}{2}$ minutes**.

The correct operation is multiplication.

Multiply $9 \times 1\frac{1}{2}$.

Change $1\frac{1}{2}$ to the improper fraction $\frac{3}{2}$ and multiply across.

$\frac{9}{1} \times \frac{3}{2} = \frac{27}{2} = 13\frac{1}{2}$ **minutes**.

17. Ilsa and Jackie spent a total of $24 at the mall. Ilsa spent $4 more than Jackie.

How much money did **each** spend?

Write your answer on the lines below.

Isla: _____

Jackie: _____

Hint #1:

Try creating a **guess and check table** and test different dollar combinations to solve this problem.

Hint #2:

Start your guess and check table by choosing two reasonable sounding dollar amounts. Because Ilsa spent **$4 dollars more** than Jackie, choose numbers that are **$4 apart**. Remember that the sum of the dollar amounts needs to be **$24**.

Answer: Ilsa spent **$14** and **Jackie** spent **$10** at the mall.

To solve this problem, you can try starting with a guess that **Ilsa spent $10** and **Jackie spent $4**. In this guess, Ilsa spent **$4** more than Jackie, but the total is **$10 + $4 = $14**. This guess is **too low**.

Next, you can try a guess that **Ilsa spent $15** and **Jackie spent $11**. These numbers are also $4 apart, but **$15 + $11 = $26**, which is **too high**.

By trying the guess that **Ilsa spent $14** and **Jackie spent $10**, you get **$14 + $10 = $24**. This is the correct combination.

18. Fred is at the movies and wants to order a drink. He can choose among **water, juice,** and **cola** and the drinks come in **3 sizes: small, medium,** and **large.**

How many different drinks does he have to choose from if he orders one drink? Write your answer on the line below.

_____

Hint #1:

Try making an **organized list** to help solve this question.

Hint #2:

Make sure your list contains each possible drink type in each of the sizes.

Answer: Fred can choose from **9 different drink combinations**.

If you made a list of all possible drink combinations, it should look something like this:

1. small water
2. small juice
3. small cola
4. medium water
5. medium juice
6. medium cola
7. large water
8. large juice
9. large cola

19. Simon painted **three rooms** in his house. Each room was a **different size**.

He used **three times** as much paint for the **second room** as he used for the **first room**.

He used **twice** as much paint for the **third room** as he used for the **second room**.

If he used **12 cans of paint** for the third room, how many cans of paint did he use for the **first room**?

Write your answer on the line below.

_____

Hint #1:

Try working **backward** to solve this problem.

Hint #2:

Start with the fact that he used 12 cans of paint for the third room and work from there.

Answer: Simon used **2 cans of paint** for the first room.

A good strategy to solve this problem is to work backward using **division**. Since Simon used **12 cans** for the **third room** and this is **twice as much** as he used for the **second room**, he used **12 ÷ 2 = 6 cans** of paint for the **second room**.

Because we know that Simon used **three times** as much paint for the **second room** as the **first room**, Simon used **6 ÷ 3 = 2 cans of paint** for the first room.

Challenge Activity

You're doing a great job so far!
Are you ready for a Challenge Activity?

Good luck!

A school is connecting the computers in a classroom.
Each computer will be connected to every other computer
with a cable.

a) If there are **3 computers**, how many **cables** will be needed?

_____

b) If **one more computer** is added, how many **cables** will
be needed?

_____

c) If there are a total of **5 computers** in the classroom,
how many **cables** will be needed?

_____

Hint #1:

It may help to make an
organized list.

Hint #2:

Start the pattern with two
computers in the room, then
continue the pattern to
3, **4**, and **5** computers.

See answers on following page.

Answers to Challenge Activity:

a) If there are 3 computers, then **3 cables** will be needed.
Label the three computers **A**, **B**, and **C**.

If there are only 2 computers, A and B, then **1 cable** will connect
computer A with computer B.

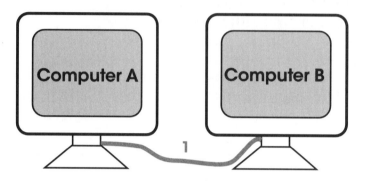

If there are 3 computers, the diagram below shows how three cables are
needed (**A** to **B**, **B** to **C**, and **C** to **A**).

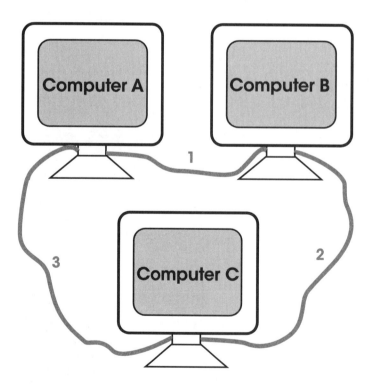

b) If one more computer is added, then **6 cables** will be needed.
One computer was added so there is a total of **4 computers**.
Continue the pattern described in part **a**.

The diagram below shows how four computers will require 6 cables (Connect **A** to **B**, **A** to **C**, **A** to **D**, **B** to **C**, **B** to **D**, and **C** to **D**):

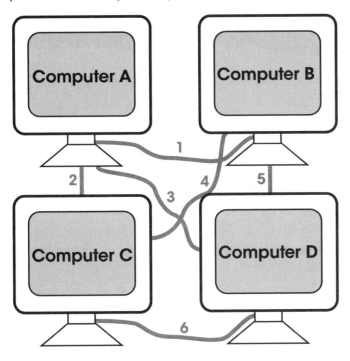

c) If there are five computers, then 10 cables would be needed.

The diagram below shows how five computers will require **10 cables** (Connect **A** to **B**, **A** to **C**, **A** to **D**, **A** to **E**, **B** to **C**, **B** to **D**, **B** to **E**, **C** to **D**, **C** to **E**, and **D** to **E**):

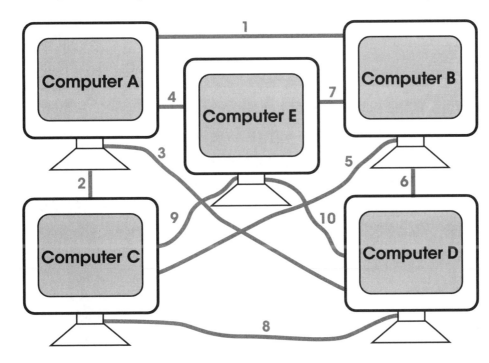

Let's take a short test and see how much you've learned during this climb up *SCORE!* Mountain.

Good luck!

1. Sally is three times as old as her brother. In two years, she will be twice as old as her brother. How old are Sally and her brother?

_____

2. Doug rakes leaves in the park during autumn and earns $7 an hour. Last week, he raked leaves for 3 hours on Monday, 2 hours on Wednesday, and 4 hours on Saturday. How much money did he earn last week?

_____

3. Jane went shopping. At the beginning of her shopping trip she spent $\frac{1}{2}$ of her money on clothes, then $24 on shoes and $22.00 on show tickets. If she had $14.00 left over at the end of the shopping trip, how much money did she start with?

_____

4. Four blocks were lined up in a row on a table. Each was a different color: red, blue, green, and yellow.

The yellow block is next to the blue block.
The green block is not next to the red block.
The row starts with a red block.
The blue block is next to the green block but not the red one.

What is the correct order of the four blocks?

_____

5. Rich, Sally, and Jon each play a different sport. The sports they play are tennis, basketball, and bowling.

Jon likes to shoot balls through a hoop.
Rich used to play tennis, but now likes to bowl.

Which sport does Sally play?

_____

See answers on following page.

Answers to test questions:

1. Sally is **6 years old** and her brother is **2 years old**.

One way to solve this problem is to use the strategy of **guess and check**. You can try your **first guess** with her brother being 5 years old. Then Sally will be **3 × 5 = 15 years old**. In two years Sally will be **15 + 2 = 17 years old** and her brother will be **5 + 2 = 7 years old**. 17 is **more** than twice as old as **7**, so try a new guess with **smaller numbers**.

You can try a **second guess** with her brother being **1 year old**. Then Sally will be **3 × 1 = 3 years old**. In two years Sally will be **3 + 2 = 5 years old** and her brother will be **1 + 2 = 3 years old**. 5 is **not** twice as old as **3**, so try a new guess with **larger numbers**.

Try a **third guess** with her brother being **2 years old**. Then Sally will be **3 × 2 = 6 years old**. In two years Sally will be **6 + 2= 8 years old** and her brother will be **2 + 2 = 4 years old**. 8 is twice as old as **4**, so **Sally is 6 and her brother is 2**.

2. Doug earned **$63** raking leaves last week.

First, determine how many total hours he worked last week: **3 + 2 + 4 = 9 hours**. You are told in the problem that Doug earns $7 an hour, so last week he earned **9 × 7 = $63**.

3. Jane started with **$120**.

Try working backward to solve this problem. Start with the **$14** she had left over. Because she spent **$22 on tickets**, add to get the amount she had before she bought the tickets: **$14 + $22 = $36**. Since she spent **$24 on shoes**, add to get the amount she had before she bought the shoes: **$36 + $24 = $60**. She spent **half** of her money on clothes at the beginning of the shopping trip. Therefore, if she had **$60** left after she bought the clothes she must have had **$60 × 2 = $120** when she started shopping.

4. The correct order of the blocks is: **red**, **yellow**, **blue**, and **green**. Try using **logical reasoning** to solve this problem.

Start with a **red block**, as indicated in the question. Because the **yellow** and **blue** blocks are next to each other, they will be either **2nd** and **3rd**, or **3rd** and **4th** in the row. The **green** block **cannot** be next to the red block, so it **must** be the **4th** block in the row. This leaves the **yellow** and **blue** blocks in the **2nd** and **3rd** positions. The **blue** block **must** be placed next to the **green** block (and not red), so it **must** be located in the **3rd** position in the row. This leaves the **yellow** block in the **2nd** position.

Answers to test questions, *continued*:

5. Sally plays **tennis**.

It may be helpful to make a table like the one below, marking an X in the boxes as they are eliminated.

	Tennis	**Basketball**	**Bowling**
Rich	X	X	✔
Sally	✔	X	X
Jon	X	✔	X

Because **Jon** likes to shoot balls through a hoop, he plays **basketball**. Place an X in the **basketball** column for the other two people, and in the **tennis** and **bowling** row for **Jon**. Because **Rich** now likes to **bowl**, the only sport left for **Sally** is **tennis**.

Celebrate!

Let's have some fun and celebrate your success! You've earned it!

Let's have a fun **picnic!**

Ask a friend or family member to join you on your picnic.

Let's plan the menu!

Make a list of the foods you would like to have on your picnic.

Congratulations!
You've made it to the top of *SCORE!* Mountain.
You did a great job!

© Kaplan Publishing, Inc.

Picnic menu

1. _____

2. _____

3. _____

4. _____

5. _____

Next, ask an adult to help you gather all the ingredients you need, put the meal together, and pack it all in a basket.

Think about some of the fun activities you'd like to do on your picnic.

You can bring along some fun games and sports equipment!

The most important thing is to have fun! You deserve it!

You should be really proud!
I knew you could make it to the top!

Here are some helpful tools to guide you through each base camp!

Use these tools whenever you need a helping hand during your climb up *SCORE!* Mountain.

Place Value: Use the chart below to determine the place value of a given number:

Each X represents a single digit from

XXX,	XXX,	XXX,	XXX,	XXX
Trillions	Billions	Millions	Thousands	Units

Within each group of three XXX, the places are named hundreds, tens and one.

Order of Operations: To evaluate a numeric or algebraic expression, use the correct order of operations, which is:

Parentheses
Exponents
Multiplication and **D**ivision, left to right
Addition and **S**ubtraction, left to right

Percent: Percent is a ratio that compares $\dfrac{part}{whole} = \dfrac{\%}{100}$

Proportion: A proportion is an equation that states that two ratios are equivalent. Proportions can be solved by cross-multiplication. If you are given a proportion such as $\dfrac{15}{100} = \dfrac{45}{n}$, cross multiply to get $15 \times n = 100 \times 45$. Then solve the equation for n, the variable term.

Perimeter: The perimeter of a figure is the sum of the lengths of the figure's sides. If the figure is on a coordinate plane, count the number of spaces to find each length.

Perimeter of a triangle: *Perimeter = side + side + side*

Perimeter of a rectangle or parallelogram:
Perimeter = 2 × length + 2 × width

Perimeter of a circle, which is called the **Circumference**:
Circumference = 2 × π × r, or *Circumference = π × d*.
In these formulas, *r* represents the **radius** and *d* represents the **diameter**. *Diameter = 2 × radius*

Similar Triangles: Similar triangles are triangles with the same shape, but different sizes. For similar triangles, the corresponding sides are in proportion.

Area: Area is the number of square units it takes to cover a figure. There are formulas to find the area of different figures:

Area of a parallelogram: *Area = base × height*

Area of a triangle: *Area = $\frac{1}{2}$ base × height*

Area of a circle: *Area = π × r²*, where *r* represents the radius of the circle.

Area of a trapezoid: *Area = $\frac{1}{2}$ (base₁ + base₂) × height*, where **base₁** and **base₂** are the lengths of the parallel sides.

Area of an Irregular-Shaped Figure: To find the area of an irregular-shaped figure, break it up into more familiar figures. Then find the area of each piece and add the areas together.

Area of a Sector of a Circle: A sector of a circle is a piece of the circle, which is formed by two radii that form a central angle:

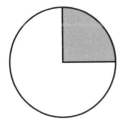

To find the area of the sector, set up a proportion reflecting $\frac{part}{whole} = \frac{part}{whole}$.

Compare the measure of the central angle to 360°, the measure of a circle. This ratio will equal the area of the sector, compared to the area of the whole circle.

Volume of a Rectangular Prism: The volume of a 3-dimensional solid is the number of cubic units it takes to fill the solid. The volume of the prism is found by using the formula:

Volume = length × width × height

Coordinate Geometry: Points and figures can lie on a coordinate plane as shown below:

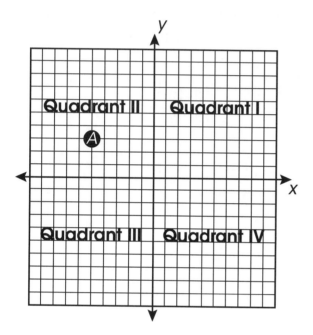

Notice that each quarter, or quadrant, is named with Roman numerals, in a counterclockwise direction. Points on a coordinate plane are located by using the form *(x,y)*.

The *x*-coordinate is the number of spaces to the left or right of the origin. If the point is to the **left** of the origin, the *x*-coordinate is **negative**, otherwise, the point is **positive** (to the right of the origin or at zero).

The *y*-coordinate is the number of spaces above or below the origin. For the *y*-coordinate, if the point is **above** the origin, the *y*-coordinate is **positive**, otherwise it is negative (below the origin or at zero).

Point A in the figure above has coordinates (−5,3).

Statistical Measures: There are four main measures used to describe a set of data:

Mean is the average value of the data set. To find the mean, find the sum of the list of data and divide by the total number of addends.

Median is the middle value in a data set. To find the median, sort the data from least to greatest and then find the middle value. If there is an even amount of data, take the average of the middle two values.

Mode is the data value that occurs most often. To find the mode, you can make a tally chart and find the value that has the most tallies. There can be one mode, no mode, or several modes.

Range is the difference between the highest and lowest values in the data set. To calculate the range, subtract: **Range = highest − lowest.**

Probability: The probability of an event happening is:
$$P(event) = \frac{\text{the number of ways the event can happen}}{\text{the total number of events}}.$$
The probability of one event and then another event is found by multiplying the probabilities together.

Problem-Solving Strategies: There are many different

Problem-Solving Strategies: There are many different problem-solving strategies that can be used to solve problems. Here are some for you to consider when attempting to solve a problem:

1. Look for a pattern
2. Make an organized list
3. Make a table
4. Choose an operation
5. Draw a picture or diagram
6. Use estimation to find a reasonable answer
7. Work backward
8. Guess and check
9. Find the unit rate
10. Use a formula

U.S. Customary Measures:

Length
> 1 foot = 12 inches
> 1 yard = 3 feet

Weight
> 1 pound = 16 ounces

Capacity
> 1 cup = 8 fluid ounces
> 1 pint = 2 cups
> 1 quart = 2 pints

Metric Measures:

Length
> 1 centimeter = 10 millimeters
> 1 meter = 100 centimeters
> 1 meter = 1,000 millimeters

Weight
> 1 kilogram = 1,000 grams

Capacity
> 1 liter = 1,000 liters

You can do it!

Use these blank pages to work out the questions in your
SCORE! Mountain Challenge Workbook.

You can do it!

You can do it!

You can do it!

You can do it!

You can do it!

You can do it!

You can do it!

You can do it!

You can do it!

You can do it!

You can do it!

You can do it!

You can do it!

You can do it!

You can do it!
No peeking!

SCORE!

Answer Hider

Tear out your answer hider and use it to cover up the answers on the bottom of every page.

Try to come up with the right answers before looking!